Manhaj al-Sālikīn wa Tawḍīḥ al Fiqh fi al Dīn

The Path of the Wayfarer and the Clarification of *Fiqh* of The Religion

Manhaj al-Sālikīn wa Tawḍīḥ al Fiqh fi al Dīn
By Sheikh ʿAbd al Raḥmān al Saʿdi

Vol.I

The Fiqh of Worship

Translated by Alomgir Ali
Tawfīq Online Learning

www.tawfiqonline.org

ISBN: 9781790110278

Edition 1.3 (January 2022)

Table of Contents

بسم الله الرحمن الرحيم

TRANSLATOR'S INTRODUCTION

Studying *fiqh* is a duty upon every believer in order to ensure that his worship is sound and correct according to the dictates of Islamic teachings. Often, we find ourselves in situations where we do not know whether certain acts have invalidated our acts of worship or whether certain aspects of our worship are recommended or obligatory etc. People then often share these concerns with others often to be confounded by a barrage of different views and opinions. Learning *fiqh* in an organised and structured manner helps a person to deal with such predicaments. It should therefore be of no surprise that having a deeper understanding of the Religion is from the signs that Allāh سبحانه وتعالى wishes good for a person. Hence, the Prophet ﷺ said, "If Allāh (swt) wishes good for someone, he grants him *fiqh* (a sound understanding) of the religion."[1] When explaining this *ḥadīth*, Ibn Ḥajar (rḥ) mentioned the following, "The implied meaning of this ḥadīth is that the one who does not learn the *fiqh* of the religion i.e. does not learn the governing principles of Islām and those subsidiary matters associated with those principles, has been denied goodness. Abū Yaʿlā narrated another weak version of the ḥadīth of Muʿāwiyah with the additional sentence, "Allāh ﷻ has no concern for the one who doesn't learn the *fiqh* of the religion." (Although weak) Its meaning is sound, since the one who does not learn the affairs of his religion and is not a scholar of *fiqh* nor a student of it, can be correctly described as being someone who good was not intended for."[2]

Manhaj al Sālikīn is a basic text that introduces the topic of *fiqh* for the layperson. It certainly will not answer all of one's *fiqh* related questions. Nevertheless, it is a good place to start from. It is a text I began translating well over a decade ago as well as it being my first major translation project and so it suffered from many shortcomings, errors and typos as one would expect. I have since gone over the translation and have had it checked by numerous friends and colleagues to try and sift out all of the errors. May I also take this opportunity to declare that all previous versions of this translation that were handed to other teachers and students

---

[1] Bukhāri

[2] *Fatḥ al Bāri* 1/165

for the purpose of their classes, are now obsolete and should not be used.

It should be noted that although the text is primarily based upon the *mathhab* of Imām Aḥmad (rḥ)[3], the author has chosen on a number of occasions to depart from the *mathhab* in favour of what he believes to be more correct. This can make it somewhat difficult for the student of the *mathhab* to deal with. For that reason, I personally believe that this text is more suited for the absolute layman who does not intend to really study *fiqh* beyond this text. In such a case, I believe this text does a good job of teaching the basic and required information that every layperson ought to know. As for the more avid seeker of knowledge, one way they can deal with this predicament is by referring to a *ḥanbalised* version of the text that was recently published by Sheikh Muḥammad ᶜAbdul Wāḥid al Ḥanbali al Azhari, "*Taḥqīq al Raghābāt bi Ḥanbalah Manhaj al Ṣālikīn wa Ziyādāt.*"[4] Otherwise, it is probably best to refer to other available texts in *ḥanbli fiqh* that have been published in English such as:

- "An Epitome of Ḥanbali Substantive Law." By Yūsuf ibn ᶜAbd al Hādi al Ḥanbali, *Dar al Arqam,* 2018.

---

[3] Sheikh al Saᶜadi wrote to his student Sheikh Ibn ᶜAqīl the following, "We have summarised it (i.e. *Manhaj al Sālikīn*) to the extent that it has become shorter than the *Mukhtaṣar* of *Al Muqniᶜ* (i.e. *Zād al Mustaqniᶜ*), *Akhṣar al Mukhtaṣarāt* and *al ᶜUmdah...*" All of these texts are standard Ḥanbali texts. See *al Ajwibah al Nāfiᶜah* p.97-98.

[4] Published by *Dār al Nūr al Mubīn,* Amman, Jordan. 2019

- "Ḥanbali Acts of Worship." From Ibn Balbān's *The Supreme Synopnis (Akhṣar al Mukhtaṣarāt), Islamosaic,* 2016.
- "Supplement for The Seeker of Certitude" Worship from *Zād al Mustaqniᶜ* by al Ḥajjāwi, *Islamosaic,* 2016.
- "Qaddūmi's Elementary Ḥanbali Primer" a translation of "*al Ajwibah al Jaliyyah fi al Aḥkām al Ḥanbaliyyah.*" 2013.
- *"Bidāyat al ᶜĀbid"* By al Baᶜli, *Two Palm Press,* 2016.
- *"Fiqh of Worship"* (from *ᶜUmdah al Fiqh* by Ibn Qudāmah), *IIPH,* 2011.

Translation of the text

I have relied on the *Dār Ibn al Jawzi* (KSA) edition, 1st print (1424h/2003). Please note that the numbering system of the text was added by the editor Muḥammad al Khuḍayri and not by Sheikh al Saᶜdi himself. Nonetheless, it was decided to keep the numbering system as it will help to break-down and study the *masāʾil* of the text. The translation only covers the section of worship. However, a second volume will be published in the near future - *inshāʾ Allāh* - covering the remaining chapters of the book.

Finally, I would like to thank all of those who helped in preparing this publication, in particular Abdus Samad Ahmed, Shaheed Uddin and everyone else who helped with the proof reading of the text.

A special mention of my wife, Umm Hanifah, has to be noted as well. Despite the many hours I spend at my desk on a daily basis, she has always been supportive of my work and considerate enough to work around my commitments. May Allāh ﷻ accept this effort and make it a means for people to learn and practice their faith.

Āmīn

Alomgir Ali
London
1st of *Ramaḍān* 1440, 6th of May 2019
Tawfīq Online Learning

THE TEXT

Introduction

All praise is due to Allāh ﷻ, we praise Him, seek His forgiveness and turn towards Him ﷻ. We seek refuge in Allāh ﷻ from the evil of our souls and the evil of our actions. Whomsoever Allāh ﷻ guides then there is none that can misguide him, and whomsoever Allāh ﷻ leads astray then there is none that can guide him. And I bear witness that there is none worthy of worship except Allāh ﷻ and I bear witness that Muḥammad ﷺ is His slave and messenger.

To proceed, this is a concise book in *al fiqh* (jurisprudence) in which I have mentioned the necessary juristic issues as well as evidences. I have limited the book so that it deals with the most important and beneficial matters in *fiqh* due to the dire need of this subject. Many times, I have simply quoted texts from the Qur'ān and Sunnah (without an explanation) if its rulings were very clear in order to make the memorisation and understanding of it easier for beginners; this is because knowledge is to have cognisance of the truth according to its evidences.

مُقدّمة

بِسْمِ اللَّهِ الرَّحْمَنِ الرَّحِيمِ

وَبِهِ نَسْتَعِين

الحَمْدُ لِلَّهِ، نَحْمَدُهُ، وَنَسْتَعِينُهُ، وَنَسْتَغْفِرُهُ، وَنَتُوبُ إِلَيْهِ، وَنَعُوذُ بِاللَّهِ مِنْ شُرُورِ أَنْفُسِنَا، وَسَيِّئَاتِ أَعْمَالِنَا، مَنْ يَهْدِ اللَّهُ فَلَا مُضِلَّ لَهُ، وَمَنْ يُضْلِلْ فَلَا هَادِيَ لَهُ، وَأَشْهَدُ أَنْ لَا إِلَهَ إِلَّا اللَّهُ، وَحْدَهُ لَا شَرِيكَ لَهُ، وَأَشْهَدُ أَنَّ مُحَمَّدًا عَبْدُهُ وَرَسُولُهُ، صَلَّى اللَّهُ عَلَيْهِ وَآلِهِ وَسَلَّمَ.

أَمَّا بَعْدُ:

فَهَذَا كِتَابٌ مُخْتَصَرٌ فِي الفِقْهِ، جَمَعْتُ فِيهِ بَيْنَ المَسَائِلِ وَالدَّلَائِلِ؛ وَاقْتَصَرْتُ فِيهِ عَلَى أَهَمِّ الأُمُورِ، وَأَعْظَمِهَا نَفْعًا، لِشِدَّةِ الضَّرُورَةِ إِلَى هَذَا المَوْضُوعِ، وَكَثِيرًا مَا أَقْتَصِرُ عَلَى النَّصِّ إِذَا كَانَ الحُكْمُ فِيهِ وَاضِحًا؛ لِسُهُولَةِ حِفْظِهِ وَفَهْمِهِ عَلَى المُبْتَدِئِينَ لِأَنَّ العِلْمَ: مَعْرِفَةُ الحَقِّ بِدَلِيلِهِ.

The definition of *fiqh* is: cognisance of the subsidiary rulings of the Sharīʿah based on the Qurʾān and Sunnah, *ijmāʿ* (consensus) and *al qiyās al ṣaḥīḥ* (correct analogy). I have also confined myself to quoting well known evidences out of fear of elongation. If a matter was disputed over, then I confined myself to mentioning the strongest opinion according to my understanding based on the proofs of the law.

1. There are 5 types of rulings (*aḥkām* pl. of *ḥukm*):

- *Wājib* (compulsory): That by which its doer is rewarded and the one who leaves it is punished.
- *Ḥarām* (prohibited): It is opposite of the above (*wājib*).
- *Makrūh* (disliked): Actions that one is rewarded for leaving but not punished for doing.
- *Masnūn* (recommended): The opposite (to *Makrūh*).
- *Mubāḥ* (permissible): An action where its doing or leaving is considered the same.

2. It is obligatory upon the *Mukallaf* (someone who is legally held accountable) to learn that which he needs for his acts of worship, transactions and other matters (in order for them to be correct).

The Prophet ﷺ said: "If Allāh ﷻ wishes good for someone He gives him *fiqh* (understanding) of the religion." (Agreed upon)

وَالْفِقْهَ: مَعْرِفَةُ الأَحْكَامِ الشَّرْعِيَّةِ الفَرْعِيَّةِ بِأَدِلَّتِهَا مِنَ الكِتَابِ، وَالسُّنَّةِ، وَالْإِجْمَاعِ، وَالْقِيَاسِ الصَّحِيحِ. وَأَقْتَصِرُ عَلَى الأَدِلَّةِ المشْهُورَةِ؛ خَوْفًا مِنَ التَّطْوِيلِ، وَإِذَا كَانَتِ المسْالَةُ خِلَافِيَّةً، اِقْتَصَرْتُ عَلَى القَوْلِ الذِي تَرَجَّحَ عِنْدِي، تَبَعًا لِلْأَدِلَّةِ الشَّرْعِيَّةِ

١. الأَحْكَامُ خَمْسَةٌ:

- الوَاجِبُ: وَهُوَ مَا أُثِيبَ فَاعِلُهُ، وَعُوقِبَ تَارِكُه.
- وَالْحَرَامُ: ضِدُّهُ.
- وَالْمَكْرُوهُ: مَا أُثِيبَ تَارِكُهُ، وَلَمْ يُعَاقَبْ فَاعِلُهُ.
- وَالْمَسْنُونُ: ضِدُّهُ.
- وَالْمُبَاحُ: وَهُوَ الذِي فِعْلُهُ وَتَرْكُهُ عَلَى حَدٍّ سَوَاءٍ.

٢. وَيَجِبُ عَلَى المكَلَّفِ أَنْ يَتَعَلَّمَ مِنْهُ كُلَّ مَا يَحْتَاجُ إِلَيْهِ فِي عِبَادَاتِهِ وَمُعَامَلَاتِهِ وَغَيْرِهَا. قَالَ ﷺ: «مَنْ يُرِدِ اللَّهُ بِهِ خَيْرًا يُفَقِّهْهُ فِي الدِّينِ.» مُتَّفَقٌ عَلَيْهِ.

كِتَابُ الطَّهَارَة

The Book of Purification

3. The Prophet ﷺ said, "Islām is built upon five; to bear witness that there is none worthy of worship except Allāh ﷻ, and that Muḥammad n is the messenger of Allāh ﷻ, establishment of the prayer, giving *zakāh*, making pilgrimage to the house and fasting Ramaḍān." (Agreed upon)

4. As for the declaration of faith, i.e. to say *lā ilāha illallāh,* then this is the knowledge of the servant of Allāh ﷻ and his firm belief and commitment to the fact that no one has the right to be worshipped except Allāh ﷻ.

This necessitates upon the servant: sincere devotion to the religion of Allāh ﷻ; that his worship, inner and outer, are all for Allāh ﷻ and that he does not associate with Allāh ﷻ anyone or anything regarding any aspect of the religion. This is the foundation of the religion of all the messengers and their followers, as Allāh ﷻ says:

"And We have not sent before you any messenger except that we revealed to him that there is no one worthy of worship except I, so worship me." (al Anbiyāʾ: 25)

كِتَابُ الطَّهَارَةِ

٣. قال النبي صلى الله عليه وسلم: «بُنِيَ الإِسْلامُ عَلَى خَمْسٍ: شَهَادَةِ أَنَّ لا إِلَهَ إِلا الله، وَأَنَّ مُحَمَّدًا رَسُولُ اللهِ، وإِقَامِ الصَّلاةِ، وَإِيتَاءِ الزَّكَاةِ، وَحِجِّ البَيتِ، وَصَومِ رَمَضَانَ». متفق عليه

٤ . فَشَهَادَةُ أَنْ لَا إِلَهَ إِلَّا اللَّهُ: عِلْمُ العَبْدِ وَاعْتِقَادِهِ وَالْتِزَامِهِ أَنَّهُ لَا يَسْتَحِقُّ الأُلُوهِيَّةَ وَالْعُبُودِيَّةَ إِلَّا اللَّهُ وَحْدَهُ لَا شَرِيكَ لَهُ.

فَيُوجِبُ ذَلِكَ عَلَى العَبْدِ: إِخْلَاصَ جَمِيعِ الدِّينِ لِلَّهِ تَعَالَى، وَأَنْ تَكُونَ عِبَادَاتُهُ الظَّاهِرَةُ وَالْبَاطِنَةُ كُلُّهَا لِلَّهِ وَحْدَهُ، وَأَنْ لَا يُشْرِكَ بِهِ شَيْئًا فِي جَمِيعِ أُمُورِ الدِّينِ.

وَهَذَا أَصْلُ دِينِ جَمِيعِ المرْسَلِينَ وَأَتْبَاعِهِمْ، كَمَا قَالَ تَعَالَى: ﴿وَمَآ أَرْسَلْنَا مِن قَبْلِكَ مِن رَّسُولٍ إِلَّا نُوحِىٓ إِلَيْهِ أَنَّهُۥ لَآ إِلَٰهَ إِلَّآ أَنَا۠ فَٱعْبُدُونِ﴾ [الأنبياء:٢٥]

5. The declaration that Muḥammad ﷺ is the Messenger of Allāh ﷻ necessitates that the servant of Allāh ﷻ firmly believes that Allāh ﷻ sent Muḥammad ﷺ to the *thaqalayn* (jinn and mankind) as a giver of glad tidings and as a warner, calling them to single out Allāh ﷻ in worship and to obey Him. It also means to believe in his (i.e. the Prophet's ﷺ) message and applying his commands and keeping away from his prohibitions. Moreover, it necessitates that one believes that there is no happiness and goodness in this world or the hereafter unless one has faith in him and follows him and that it is an obligation to put the love of him above the love of oneself, children and all of mankind.

It also implies that one believes that Allāh ﷻ provided the Prophet ﷺ with miracles to prove his message; that Allāh ﷻ endowed him with knowledge and a noble character; that his religion is one of guidance, mercy and truth; and that it entails both religious and worldly benefit.

The greatest sign of Allāh ﷻ is the Qurʾān. It embodies the truth in what it relates as well as its commandments and prohibitions.

And Allāh ﷻ knows best.

٥. وَشَهَادَةُ أَنَّ مُحَمَّدًا رَسُولُ اللَّهِ: أَنْ يَعْتَقِدَ العَبْدُ أَنَّ اللَّهَ أَرْسَلَ مُحَمَّدًا ﷺ إِلَى جَمِيعِ الثَّقَلَيْنِ - الإِنْسِ وَالْجِنِّ - بَشِيراً وَنَذِيرًا, يَدْعُوهُمْ إِلَى تَوْحِيدِ اللَّهِ وَطَاعَتِهِ, بِتَصْدِيقِ خَبَرِهِ, وَامْتِثَالِ أَمْرِهِ, وَاجْتِنَابِ نَهْيِهِ, وَأَنَّهُ لَا سَعَادَةَ وَلَا صَلَاحَ فِي الدُّنْيَا وَالْآخِرَةِ إِلَّا بِالْإِيمَانِ بِهِ وَطَاعَتِهِ, وَأَنَّهُ يَجِبُ تَقْدِيمُ مَحَبَّتِهِ عَلَى مَحَبَّةِ النَّفْسِ وَالْوَلَدِ وَالنَّاسِ أَجْمَعِينَ.

وَأَنَّ اللَّهَ أَيَّدَهُ بِالْمُعْجِزَاتِ الدَّالَّةِ عَلَى رِسَالَتِهِ، وَبِمَا جَبَلَهُ اللَّهُ عَلَيْهِ مِنَ العُلُومِ الكَامِلَةِ، وَالْأَخْلَاقِ العَالِيَةِ، وَبِمَا اِشْتَمَلَ عَلَيْهِ دَيْنُهُ مِنَ الهُدَى وَالرَّحْمَةِ وَالحَقِّ، وَالْمَصَالِحِ الدِّينِيَّةِ وَالدُّنْيَوِيَّةِ

وَآيَتُهُ الكُبْرَى: هَذَا القُرْآنُ العَظِيمُ، بِمَا فِيهِ مِنَ الحَقِّ فِي الأَخْبَارِ وَالْأَمْرِ وَالنَّهْيِ، وَاللَّهُ أَعْلَمُ.

فَصْل

(في المِيَاه)

Chapter: Water

6. The prayer has conditions (*shurūṭ* pl. of *sharṭ*) that precede it, amongst them:

7. Ritual purification (*ṭahārah*). The Prophet ﷺ said, "Allāh ﷻ does not accept a prayer without purification." (Agreed upon) Thus, the one who does not purify himself from ritual impurity, major and minor, as well as physical impurities, will render his prayer invalid.

8. There are two methods of purification (*ṭahārah*):

9. The first is purification by water, this is the primary method of purification.

10. All water that descends from the sky or comes out from the ground is purifying (*ṭahūr*). Such water purifies one from ritual impurities (*ḥadath*) as well as physical (*khabath*) even if its colour, taste or smell was changed by something pure since the Prophet ﷺ said, "Verily water is pure, and nothing makes it impure." (Abū Dāwūd & Tirmidhi)

فَصْلٌ

فِي المِيَاهِ

٦. وَأَمَّا الصَّلَاةُ: فَلَهَا شُرُوطٌ تَتَقَدَّمُ عَلَيْهَا.

فَمِنْهَا:

٧. الطَّهَارَةُ: كَمَا قَالَ النَّبِيُّ ﷺ: «لَا يَقْبَلُ اللّٰهُ صَلَاةً بِغَيْرِ طَهُورٍ.» مُتَّفَقٌ عَلَيْهِ. فَمَنْ لَمْ يَتَطَهَّرْ مِنَ الحَدَثِ الأَكْبَرِ وَالأَصْغَرِ وَالنَّجَاسَةِ فَلَا صَلَاةَ لَهُ.

٨. وَالطَّهَارَةُ نَوْعَانِ:

٩. الطَّهَارَةُ بِالمَاءِ، وَهِيَ الأَصْلُ

١٠. فَكُلُّ مَاءٍ نَزَلَ مِنَ السَّمَاءِ، أَوْ نَبَعَ مِنْ الأَرْضِ، فَهُوَ طَهُورٌ، يُطَهِّرُ مِنَ الأَحْدَاثِ وَالأَخْبَاثِ. وَلَوْ تَغَيَّرَ لَوْنُهُ أَوْ طَعْمُهُ أَوْ رِيحُهُ بِشَيْءٍ طَاهِرٍ، كَمَا قَالَ النَّبِيُّ ﷺ: «إِنَّ المَاءَ طَهُورٌ لَا يُنَجِّسُهُ شَيْءٌ.» رَوَاهُ أَهْلُ السُّنَنِ وَهُوَ صَحِيحٌ.

11. If one of its three characteristics changes by something impure, then it is considered to be *najis* (impure); thus, it is compulsory to keep away from it (i.e., one cannot use it for purification).

12. The original ruling of things is that they are pure and permissible to use.

13. Thus, if one doubts the purity of water, clothes, surface or anything else, it is considered *ṭāhir* (pure). Likewise, if one was sure that they were initially in a state of purification and then doubted whether they preserved their purification, they are also *ṭāhir* (pure) due to the statement of the Prophet ﷺ to the person who imagined to have passed wind during prayer, "One should not leave (his *ṣalāh*) until he hears a sound or finds a smell." (Agreed upon)

١١. فَإِنْ تَغَيَّرَ أَحَدُ أَوْصَافِهِ بِنَجَاسَةٍ فَهُوَ نَجِسٌ، يَجِبُ اِجْتِنَابُه.

١٢. والأَصْلُ فِي الأَشْيَاء: الطَّهَارَةُ والإِبَاحَةُ

١٣. فَإِذَا شَكَّ المسْلِمُ فِي نَجَاسَةِ مَاءٍ أَوْ ثَوْبٍ أَوْ بُقْعَةٍ، أَوْ غَيْرِهَا: فَهُوَ طَاهِرٌ، أَوْ تَيَقَّنَ الطَّهَارَةَ وَشَكَّ فِي الحَدَثِ: فَهُوَ طَاهِرٌ; لِقَوْلِهِ صلى اللهُ عَليه وسَلَّمَ فِي الرَّجُلِ يُخَيَّلُ إِلَيْهِ أَنَّهُ يَجِدُ الشَّيْءَ فِي الصَّلَاةِ: «لَا يَنْصَرِفْ حَتَّى يَسْمَعَ صَوْتًا أَوْ يَجِدَ رِيحًا.» مُتَّفَقٌ عَلَيْهِ

بَابُ الآنِيَة

Chapter: Utensils

14. All utensils are permissible.

15. Except gold and silver utensils and that which contains them, except for a small amount of silver due to a pressing need (*ḥājah*). This is due to the statement of the Prophet ﷺ, "Do not drink from containers made of gold and silver and do not eat from its (gold and silver) bowls, for verily it is for them in this world and for us in the Afterlife." (Agreed upon)

بَابُ الاسْتِنْجَاءِ وآدَاب قَضَاءِ الحَاجَة

Chapter: *Istinjāʾ* and the Etiquettes of Relieving Oneself

16. It is recommended that if one enters an area to relieve oneself that one enters with their left foot (before their right) and says:

بِسْمِ اللهِ اللَّهُمَّ إِنِّي أَعُوذُ بِكَ مِنَ الخُبثِ والخَبَائِث

Bismillāh, Allāhumma innī aʿūdhu bika minal khubthi/khubuthi wal khabāʾith

"In the name of Allāh, O Allāh! I seek refuge in you from male & female devils."

بَابُ الآنِيَةِ

١٤ . وَجَمِيعُ الأَوَانِي مُبَاحَةٌ.

١٥ . إِلَّا آنِيَةَ الذَّهَبِ وَالْفِضَّةِ وَمَا فِيهِ شَيْءٌ مِنْهُمَا، إِلَّا اليَسِيرَ مِنْ الفِضَّةِ لِلْحَاجَةِ لِقَوْلِهِ ﷺ: «لَا تَشْرَبُوا فِي آنِيَةِ الذَّهَبِ وَالْفِضَّةِ، وَلَا تَأْكُلُوا فِي صِحَافِهَا فَإِنَّهَا لَهُمْ فِي الدُّنْيَا، وَلَكُمْ فِي الآخِرَةِ.» مُتَّفَقٌ عَلَيْهِ.

بَابُ الاسْتِنْجَاءِ وَآدَابِ قَضَاءِ الحَاجَةِ

١٦ . يُسْتَحَبُّ إِذَا دَخَلَ الخَلَاءَ: أَنْ يَقْدَمَ رِجْلَهُ اليُسْرَى، وَيَقُولَ: بِسْمِ اللَّهِ، اللَّهُمَّ إِنِّي أَعُوذُ بِكَ مِنْ الخُبْثِ وَالْخَبَائِثِ

17. And when one leaves, one should:

1. leave with their right foot
2. say,

غُفْرَانَكَ

Ghufrānaka

"O Allāh, I seek your forgiveness"

الحَمْدُ للهِ الَّذِي أَذْهَبَ عَنِّي الأَذَى وَعَافَانِي

al ḥamdulillāhil-ladhī adh-haba ʾannil athā wa ʿāfānī

"Praise is to Allah ﷻ Who has relieved me of impurity and given me good health."

18. One should support themselves by putting more weight on their left leg and erecting their right.

19. One should conceal themselves with a barrier or by something else.

20. One should distance themselves away from people if one was in an open area.

١٧. وَإِذَا خَرَجَ مِنْهُ:

- قَدَّمَ اليُمْنى
- وَقَالَ: غُفْرَانَكَ
- الحَمْدُ لِلَّهِ الذِي أَذْهَبَ عَنِّي الأَذَى وَعَافَانِي.

١٨. وَيَعْتَمِدُ فِي جُلُوسِهِ عَلَى رِجْلِهِ اليُسْرَى، وَيَنْصِبُ اليُمْنَى

١٩. وَيَسْتَتِرُ بِحَائِطٍ أَوْ غَيْرِهِ

٢٠. وَيَبْعُدُ إِنْ كَانَ فِي الفَضَاءِ

21. It is not permissible to answer the call of nature in:

1. Pathways
2. Places where people sit.
3. Underneath trees that give fruit.
4. Or in an area that will harm other people.

22. It is not permitted to face the *qiblah* or turn one's back to it while relieving oneself due to the saying of the Prophet ﷺ, "If anyone of you goes to an open space for answering the call of nature, he should neither face nor turn his back towards the *qiblah* while urinating or defecating. Instead, he should face the east or west." (Agreed upon)

23. After relieving oneself, one should:

1. Do *Istijmār* (cleaning the private parts by using a solid material) with three stones or something similar to it that cleans the required area.
2. Then one should do *istinjā*ʿ (cleaning the private parts with water until the impurity is washed away)

٢١. وَلا يَحِلُّ لَهُ أَنْ يَقْضِيَ حَاجَتَهُ في

- طَرِيقٍ
- أَوْ مَحَلِّ جُلُوسِ النَّاس
- أَوْ تَحْتِ الأَشْجَارِ المثْمِرَةِ
- أَوْ في مَحَلٍّ يُؤْذِي بِهِ النَّاسَ

٢٢. وَلَا يَسْتَقْبِلُ القِبْلَةَ أَوْ يَسْتَدْبِرُهَا حَالَ قَضَاءِ الحَاجَةِ لِقَوْلِهِ: "إِذَا أَتَيْتُمُ الغَائِطَ فَلَا تَسْتَقْبِلُوا القِبْلَةَ بِغَائِطٍ وَلَا بَوْلٍ، وَلَا تَسْتَدْبِرُوهَا، وَلَكِنْ شَرِّقُوا أَوْ غَرِّبُوا." مُتَّفَقٌ عَلَيْهِ

٢٣. فَإِذَا قَضَى حَاجَتَهُ:

- اِسْتَجْمَرَ بِثَلَاثَةِ أَحْجَارٍ وَنَحْوِهَا، تُنَقِّي المحَلَّ.
- ثُمَّ اِسْتَنْجَى بِالماءِ

24. It is sufficient to restrict oneself to one of the two (i.e. *istijmār* or *istinjāʿ*)

25. One cannot perform *istijmār* with the following:

1. Dung or bones, as that was prohibited by the Prophet ﷺ.
2. Anything of sanctity.

٢٤. وَيَكْفِي الاِقْتِصَارُ عَلَى أَحَدِهِمَا.

٢٥. وَلاَ يُسْتَجْمَرُ:

- بِالرَوَثِ والعظام، لنهي النبي صَلى الله عَلَيْهِ وسلَّم عن ذلك،

- وكَذَلِكَ كُلُّ مَا لَهُ حُرْمَةِ.

فَصْل

إِزَالَةُ النَّجَاسَةِ والأَشْيَاء النَّجسَة

Chapter: The Removal of Impurities and an Account of Impure Substances

26. It is sufficient to wash all impurities whether they were on the body, clothes, the area (one prays in) or any other area by removing the impurity itself from the area. This is because the legislator did not stipulate for the washing of all impurities a specific amount of washes, except in the case of the impurity of a dog, since the legislator stipulated for the washing of the impurity of the dog seven washes, one by earth, as in the *ḥadīth* which is agreed upon.

27. The following things are impure:

1. Human urine

2. Human faeces

3. Blood, except for a small amount as that is excused. An example (of impure blood) is blood that has been spilt from slaughtering animals that are permissible to eat, except for the blood that remains in the meat and veins for that is pure.

فَصْلٌ

إِزَالَةُ النَّجَاسَةِ وَالْأَشْيَاءِ النَّجِسَةِ

٢٦. وَيَكْفِي فِي غَسْلِ جَمِيعِ النَّجَاسَاتِ عَلَى البَدَنِ، أَوْ الثَّوْبِ، أَوْ البُقْعَةِ، أَوْ غَيْرِهَا: أَنْ تَزُولَ عَيْنُهَا عَنِ المَحَلِّ. لِأَنَّ الشَّارِعَ لَمْ يَشْتَرِطْ فِي جَمِيعِ غَسْلِ النَّجَاسَاتِ عَدَدًا إِلَّا فِي نَجَاسَةِ الكَلْبِ، فَاشْتَرَطَ فِيهَا سَبْعَ غَسْلَاتٍ، إِحْدَاهَا بِالتُّرَابِ فِي الحَدِيثِ المُتَّفَقِ عَلَيْهِ.

٢٧. وَالْأَشْيَاءُ النَّجِسَةُ

١- بَوْلُ الآدَمِيِّ.

٢- وَعُذْرَتُهُ.

٣- وَالدَّمُ، إِلَّا أَنَّهُ يُعْفَى عَنِ الدَّمِ اليَسِيرِ. وَمِثْلُهُ: الدَّمُ المَسْفُوحُ مِنْ الحَيَوَانِ المَأْكُولِ، دُونَ الذِي يَبْقَى فِي اللَّحْمِ وَالْعُرُوقِ. فَإِنَّهُ طَاهِرٌ.

4. The urine and faeces of every animal that is impermissible to eat.

5. All predators

6. Likewise, all dead animals that were not slaughtered according to ritual requirements, except for dead humans and that which does not have flowing blood (e.g. flies, mosquitoes), fish and locust, since they are pure.

Allāh ﷻ says in the Qurʾān, "*You are forbidden to eat carrion; blood; pig's meat; any animal over which any name other than God's has been invoked; any animal strangled, or victim of a violent blow or a fall, or gored or savaged by a beast of prey, unless you still slaughter it [in the correct manner]; or anything sacrificed on idolatrous altars...*" (5: 3)

The Prophet said ﷺ, "The believer does not become impure while alive or dead." (Agreed upon).

He ﷺ also said, "Two types of carrion and blood have been made permissible. As for the two types of carrion, (they are) fish and locust. As for the two types of blood, (they are blood from) the liver and spleen." (Aḥmād and ibn Mājah)

28. The faeces and urine of animals that are permissible to eat are pure.

٤- وَمِنَ النَّجَاسَاتِ: بَوْلُ وَرَوْثُ كُلِّ حَيَوَانٍ مُحَرَّمٍ أَكْلُهُ.

٥- وَالسِّبَاعُ كُلُّهَا نَجِسَةٌ

٦- وَكَذَلِكَ الميتات، إِلَّا: مَيْتَةَ الآدَمِيِّ، وَمَا لَا نَفْسَ لَهُ سَائِلَة

وَالسَّمَكَ وَالْجَرَادَ ; لِأَنَّهَا طَاهِرَةٌ.

قَالَ تَعَالَى: ﴿حُرِّمَتْ عَلَيْكُمُ الْمَيْتَةُ وَالدَّمُ...﴾ إِلَى آخِرِهَا [المائدة: ٣]

وَقَالَ النَّبِيُّ ﷺ: «المؤْمِنُ لَا يَنْجُسُ حَيًّا وَلَا مَيِّتًا»

وَقَالَ: «أُحِلَّ لَنَا مَيْتَتَانِ وَدَمَانِ، أَمَا الْمَيْتَتَانِ: فَالْحُوتُ وَالْجَرَادُ. وَأَمَّا الدَّمَانِ: فَالْكَبِدُ وَالطِّحَالُ.» رَوَاهُ أَحْمَدُ وَابْنُ مَاجه.

٢٨. وَأَمَّا أَرْوَاثُ الحَيَوَانَاتِ المأْكُولَةِ وَأَبْوَالُهَا: فَهِيَ طَاهِرَةٌ.

29. *Maniyy* (semen) of a human is pure. The Prophet ﷺ used to wash it from his clothes when it i.e. the sperm was moist and would scrape it off his clothes when it was dry.

30. It is sufficient to sprinkle water on the urine of a baby boy that does not eat solid food out of desire for it since the Prophet ﷺ said: "The urine of a baby girl is to be washed and the urine of a baby boy is to be sprinkled over." (Abū Dāwūd and Nasāʾi)

31. If the impure substance is removed from the affected area then the area is pure. Any residual colour or smell does not affect the ruling. This is due to the statement of the Prophet ﷺ to Khalwah رضي الله عنها regarding the blood of menstruation, "Water suffices you and its effects (from the blood) will not harm you." (Abū Dāwūd & Aḥmad)

٢٩. ومني الآدمي طاهر، كان النبي صلى الله عليه وسلم يَغْسِلُ رَطْبَهُ، وَيَفْرُكُ يَابِسَهُ

٣٠. وبَوْلُ الغُلَامِ الصَّغِيرِ، الذِي لَمْ يَأْكُلِ الطَّعَامَ لِشَهْوَةٍ: يَكْفِي فِيهِ النَّضْحُ. كَمَا قَالَ النَّبِيُّ ﷺ: «يُغْسَلُ مِنْ بَوْلِ الجَارِيَةِ، وَيُرَشُّ مِنْ بَوْلِ الغُلَامِ.» رَوَاهُ أَبُو دَاوُدَ وَالنَّسَائِيُّ.

٣١. وَإِذَا زَالَتْ عَيْنُ النَّجَاسَةِ طَهُرَ المحَلُّ وَلَمْ يَضُرَّ بَقَاءُ اللَّوْنِ وَالرِّيحِ; لِقَوْلِهِ صَلَّى اللهُ عَلَيْهِ وسَلَّمَ لِخَوْلَةَ فِي دَمِ الحَيْضِ «يَكْفِيكِ الماءُ، وَلَا يَضُرُّكِ أَثَرُهُ.»

بَابُ صِفَةِ الوُضُوءِ

Chapter: The Description of Ablution

32. The ablution is performed by:

1. Intending the removal of *ḥadath* (ritual impurity) or intending ablution for prayer etc.

The intention is a *sharṭ* (condition) for all actions of purification and other than it.

2. Then to say: *Bismillāh*

3. Then to wash the hands until the wrists three times.

4. Then to do *maḍmaḍah* (taking water into the mouth and then expelling it) and *istinshāq* (taking water into the nose and then expelling it) three times with three handfuls of water.

5. Then to wash the face three times.

6. Then the arms until the elbows.

7. Then, to wipe the entire head with both hands once. Starting from the beginning of the head up until the nape, and then returning back to the beginning of the head. This is to be done one time.

بَابُ صِفَةِ الوُضُوءِ

٣٢. وَهُوَ:

١- أَنْ يَنْوِيَ رَفْعَ الحَدَثِ، أَوْ الوُضُوءَ لِلصَّلَاةِ وَنَحْوِهَا.

وَالنِّيَّةُ: شَرْطٌ لِجَمِيعِ الأَعْمَالِ مِنْ طَهَارَةٍ وَغَيْرِهَا؛ لِقَوْلِهِ ﷺ: «إِنَّمَا الأَعْمَالُ بِالنِّيَّاتِ، وَإِنَّمَا لِكُلِّ امْرِئٍ مَا نَوَى.» مُتَّفَقٌ عَلَيْهِ.

٢- ثُمَّ يَقُولُ: «بِسْمِ اللَّهِ».

٣- وَيَغْسِلُ كَفَّيْهِ ثَلَاثًا.

٤- ثُمَّ يَتَمَضْمَضُ وَيَسْتَنْشِقُ ثَلَاثًا، بِثَلَاثِ غَرْفَاتٍ.

٥- ثُمَّ يَغْسِلُ وَجْهَهُ ثَلَاثًا.

٦- وَيَدَيْهِ إِلَى المِرْفَقَيْنِ ثَلَاثًا.

٧- وَيَمْسَحُ رَأْسَهُ مِنْ مُقَدَّمِ رَأْسِهِ إِلَى قَفَاهُ بِيَدَيْهِ. ثُمَّ يُعِيدُهُمَا إِلَى المَحَلِّ الذي بَدَأَ مِنْهُ مَرَّةً وَاحِدَةً.

8. Then to insert one's index fingers into the ears and to wipe the outer part of the ear with the thumb.

9. Then to wash the feet (including the ankles) three times each.

This is the most complete way of performing the ablution.

33. The obligatory parts of the ablution are:

1. To wash (each limb) once.

2. To perform the actions of ablution in the order (*tartīb*) described in the verse, "*O you who believe! When you rise to perform prayer, wash your faces and your forearms to the elbows and wipe over your heads and wash your feet to the ankles...*" (5: 6)

3. To wash each limb in succession, such that there isn't a customary long gap between the washing of different limbs. This holds true for everything that stipulates *muwālāh* (matters to be done consecutively without a long gap).

٨- ثُمَّ يَدْخُلَ سَبَّاحَتَيْهِ فِي صِمَاخَيْ أُذُنَيْهِ، وَيَمْسَح بِإِبْهَامَيْهِ ظَاهِرَهُمَا.

٩- ثُمَّ يَغْسِلَ رِجلَيْهِ مَعَ الكَعْبَيْنِ ثَلَاثًا ثَلَاثًا.

هَذَا أَكْمَلُ الوُضُوءِ الذِي فَعَلَهُ النَّبِيُّ ﷺ.

٣٣. وَالْفَرْضُ مِنْ ذَلِكَ:

١- أَنْ يَغْسِلَ مَرَّةً وَاحِدَةً.

٢- وَأَنْ يُرَتِّبَهَا عَلَى مَا ذَكَرَهُ اللَّهُ تَعَالَى فِي قَوْلِهِ: ﴿يَٰٓأَيُّهَا ٱلَّذِينَ ءَامَنُوٓاْ إِذَا قُمْتُمْ إِلَى ٱلصَّلَوٰةِ فَٱغْسِلُواْ وُجُوهَكُمْ وَأَيْدِيَكُمْ إِلَى ٱلْمَرَافِقِ وَٱمْسَحُواْ بِرُءُوسِكُمْ وَأَرْجُلَكُمْ إِلَى ٱلْكَعْبَيْنِ﴾ [المائدة: ٦]

٣- وَأَنْ لَا يَفْصِلَ بَيْنَهَا بِفَاصِلٍ طَوِيلٍ عُرْفًا، بِحَيْثُ لَا يَنْبَنِي بَعْضُهُ عَلَى بَعْضٍ، وَكَذَا كُلُّ مَا اشْتُرِطَتْ لَهُ المُوَالَاةُ.

فَصْل
فِي الْمَسْحِ عَلَى الخُفَّيْن والجَبِيرَة
Chapter: Wiping of Footwear and Bandages

34. If one is wearing two *khuffs* or something similar to them, he can wipe over them if he wishes:

1. For one day and night if one is a *muqīm* (resident) and for three days and three nights if one is a *musāfir* (traveller).

2. With the condition that he wore the footwear while in a state of *ṭahārah* (purification).

3. One can only wipe over them if in a state of minor ritual impurity (*al ḥadath al aṣghar*).

It was reported on the authority of Anas ﷺ that the Prophet ﷺ said, "If one of you performs ablution and puts on his footwear, let him wipe over them and pray in them, and he doesn't have to remove them except due to *janābah* (i.e. sexual impurity)." (al Ḥākim)

35. If one has a bandage or medicine on a limb that is usually washed during ablution, and washing it would be harmful, then one can wipe over it for both minor and major ritual impurity until the wound has healed.

فَصْلٌ

فِي المَسْحِ عَلَى الخُفَّيْنِ وَالجَبِيرَةِ

٣٤. فَإِنْ كَانَ عَلَيْهِ خُفَّانِ وَنَحْوُهُمَا مَسْح عَلَيْهِمَا إِنْ شَاءَ

١. يَوْمًا وَلَيْلَةً لِلْمُقِيمِ وَثَلَاثَةَ أَيَّامٍ بِلَيَالِيهِنَّ لِلْمُسَافِرِ.

٢. بِشَرْطِ أَنْ يَلْبَسَهُمَا عَلَى طَهَارَةٍ.

٣. وَلَا يَمْسَحهُمَا إِلَّا فِي الحَدَثِ الأَصْغَرِ.

عن أنس مرفوعًا: «إِذَا تَوَضَّأَ أَحَدُكُمْ، وَلَبِسَ خُفَّيْهِ فَلْيَمْسَحْ عَلَيهِمَا، ولْيُصَلِّ فِيهِمَا، ولا يَخْلَعْهُمَا إِنْ شَاءَ إلا مِنْ جَنَابَةٍ.» رَوَاهُ الحَاكِمُ وَصَحَّحَهُ.

٣٥. فَإِنْ كَانَ عَلَى أَعْضَاءِ وَضُوئِهِ جَبِيرَةٌ عَلَى كَسْرٍ، أَوْ دَوَاءٌ عَلَى جُرْحٍ، وَيَضُرُّهُ الغُسْلُ: مَسَحَهُ بِالْمَاءِ فِي الحَدَثِ الأَكْبَرِ وَالْأَصْغَرِ حَتَّى يَبْرَأَ.

36. The method of wiping over footwear is to wipe most of its upper part.

37. As for the *jabīrah* (bandage/cast), then one should wipe over all of it.

٣٦. وَصِفَةُ مَسَحِ الخُفَّيْنِ: أَنْ يَمْسَحَ أَكْثَرَ ظَاهِرِهِمَا.

٣٧. وَأَمَّا الجَبِيرَةُ: فَيَمْسَحُ عَلَى جَمِيعِهَا.

بَابُ نَوَاقِضِ الوُضُوءِ

Chapter: Nullifiers of Ablution

38. The nullifiers of ablution are:

1. Anything that leaves the body via the private parts.

2. A large amount of blood (exiting the body) and its like (i.e. other impurities).

3. The loss of consciousness (or sanity) by sleep or any other cause.

4. Eating camel meat.

5. Touching the opposite gender with desire.

6. Touching the private parts.

7. Washing a dead person.

8. Apostasy, which also nullifies all of one's good deeds.

This is due to the saying of Allāh ﷻ, "*...or one of you comes from the place of relieving oneself or you have touched women.*" (5:5)

بَابُ نَوَاقِضِ الوُضُوءِ

٣٨. وَهِيَ:

١- الخَارِجُ مِنْ السَّبِيلَيْنِ مُطْلَقًا.

٢- وَالدَّمُ الكَثِيرُ وَنَحْوُهُ.

٣- وَزَوَالُ العَقْلِ بِنَوْمٍ أَوْ غَيْرِهِ.

٤- وَأَكَلُ لَحْمِ الجَزُورِ.

٥- وَمَسُّ المَرْأَةِ بِشَهْوَةٍ.

٦- وَمَسُّ الفَرْجِ.

٧- وَتَغْسِيلُ المَيِّتِ.

٨- وَالرِّدَّةُ: وَهِيَ تُحْبِطُ الأَعْمَالَ كُلَّهَا.

لِقَوْلِهِ تَعَالَى: ﴿أَوْ جَآءَ أَحَدٌ مِّنكُم مِّنَ ٱلْغَآئِطِ أَوْ لَـٰمَسْتُمُ ٱلنِّسَآءَ﴾ [المائدة: ٦]

The Prophet ﷺ was asked, “Should we do ablution after eating camel meat?” so He said, “Yes”. (Muslim)

He also said regarding the two *khuffs,* “The Messenger of Allāh ﷺ would not command us not to take off our leather socks for three days except in the case of sexual impurity, but not in the case of defecation, urine or sleep” (i.e. during travel) (Tirmidhi and Nasā’i).

وَسُئِلَ النَّبِيُّ ﷺ: «أَنَتَوَضَّأُ مِنْ لُحُومِ الإِبِلِ؟ فَقَالَ: نَعَمْ.» رَوَاهُ مُسْلِمٌ.

وَقَالَ فِي الخُفَّيْنِ: «وَلَكِنْ مِنْ غَائِطٍ وَبَوْلٍ وَنَوْم.» رَوَاهُ النَّسَائِيُّ وَالتِّرْمِذِيُّ وَصَحَّحَهُ

بَابُ مَا يُوجِبُ الغُسْلِ وصِفَته

Chapter: That Which Obligates *Ghusl* and the Manner of Performing It.

39. *Ghusl* becomes obligatory from the following matters:

1. *Janābah* (sexual defilement), which results from:

A. The ejaculation of *maniyy* (semen) due to intercourse or any other means.
B. When the two circumcised parts meet.

2. Menstruation or post-natal bleeding.

3. Death, excluding a martyr.

4. When a disbeliever embraces Islām.

Allāh ﷻ says in the Qur'ān: *"...and if you are in the state of janābah then purify yourselves."* (Mā'idah: 6).

Allāh ﷻ says in the Qur'ān: *"...and do not approach them until they purify themselves. And if they purified themselves approach them from where Allah has ordained for you."* (Baqarah: 222). I.e. if they performed *ghusl.*

The Prophet ﷺ ordered the one who washed the dead to do *ghusl* himself.

بَابُ مَا يُوجِبُ الغُسْلَ وَصِفَتِهِ

٣٩. وَيَجِبُ الغُسْلُ مِنَ:

١- الجَنَابَةِ: وَهِيَ:

أَ- إِنْزَالُ المنِيِّ بِوَطْءٍ أَوْ غَيْرِهِ.

بِ- أَوْ بِالْتِقَاءِ الخِتَانَيْنِ.

٢- وخُرُوجِ دَمِ الحَيْضِ، والنِّفَاسِ

٣ - ومَوْتِ غَيْرِ الشَّهِيدِ

٤ - وَإِسْلامِ الكَافِرِ.

قال تعالى: ﴿وَإِن كُنتُمۡ جُنُبٗا فَٱطَّهَّرُواْۚ﴾ [المائدة: ٦]

وقال تعالى: ﴿وَلَا تَقۡرَبُوهُنَّ حَتَّىٰ يَطۡهُرۡنَۖ فَإِذَا تَطَهَّرۡنَ فَأۡتُوهُنَّ مِنۡ حَيۡثُ أَمَرَكُمُ ٱللَّهُۚ﴾ [البقرة: ٢٢٢] أي :إذا اِغْتَسَلْنَ

وقد أمر النبي صلى الله عليه وسلم بِالْغُسْلِ مِنْ تَغْسِيلِ المَيِّتِ.

He also ordered for the one who embraced Islam to perform the *ghusl.*

40. As for the method in which the Prophet ﷺ performed the *ghusl* from *janābah:*

1. He would wash his private part first.

2. Then he would perform a complete ablution.

3. Then he would pour water on his head three times, making sure that the water reached his scalp.

4. Then he would pour water over the rest of his body.

5. Then he would wash his feet in another area.

41. The obligatory parts of *ghusl* are to wash the entire body and the roots of one's hair whether their hair is thick or not. And Allāh ﷻ knows best.

وَأَمَرَ مَنْ أَسْلَمَ أَنْ يَغْتَسِلَ

٤٠. وَأَمَّا صِفَةُ غَسْلِ النَّبِيِّ ﷺ مِنَ الجَنَابَةِ:

١. فَكَانَ يَغْسِلُ فَرْجَهُ أَوَّلًا.

٢. ثُمَّ يَتَوَضَّأُ وُضُوءًا كَامِلًا.

٣. ثُمَّ يَحْثِي الماءِ عَلَى رَأْسِهِ ثَلَاثًا، يَرْوِيهِ بِذَلِكَ.

٤. ثُمَّ يُفِيضُ الْمَاءَ عَلَى سَائِرِ جَسَدِهِ.

٥. ثُمَّ يَغْسِلُ رِجْلَيْهِ بِمَحَلٍّ آخَر

٤١. وَالْفَرْضُ مِنْ هَذَا: غَسْلُ جَمِيعِ البَدَنِ، وَمَا تَحْتَ الشُّعُورِ الخَفِيفَةِ وَالْكَثِيفَةِ. وَاللَّهُ أَعْلَمَ.

بَابُ التَّيَمُّم

Chapter: *Tayammum*

42. It is the second method of purification.

43. It is used as a substitute of water if the usage of water (that is required to wash the required areas in ablution or some of the areas) becomes unfeasible due to its unavailability or fear of harm due to its usage.

44. *Turāb* (earth) will take the place of water by:

1. Intending to remove the ritual state of impurity (*aḥdāth* pl. of *ḥadath*).

2. Then saying, "*Bismillāh.*"

3. Then striking the earth with one's hands one time.

4. Then wiping the face with both hands and then wiping the hands.

45. There is no harm in striking the earth twice.

بَابُ التَّيَمُّمِ

٤٢. وَهُوَ النَّوْعُ الثَّانِي مِنَ الطَّهَارَةِ.

٤٣. وَهُوَ بَدَلٌ عَنِ الماءِ إِذَا تَعَذَّرَ اِسْتِعْمَالُ الماءِ لِأَعْضَاءِ الطَّهَارَةِ أَوْ بَعْضِهَا لِعَدَمِهِ، أَوْ خَوْفِ ضَرَرٍ بِاسْتِعْمَالِهِ.

٤٤. فَيَقُومُ التُّرَابُ مَقَامَ الماءِ بِأَنْ:

١. يَنْوِيَ رَفْعَ مَا عَلَيْهِ مِنْ الأَحْدَاثِ.

٢. ثُمَّ يَقُولُ بِسْمِ اللَّهِ.

٣. ثُمَّ يَضْرِبَ التُّرَابَ بِيَدِهِ مَرَّةً وَاحِدَةً.

٤. يَمْسَحُ بِهِمَا جَمِيعَ وَجْهِهِ وَجَمِيعَ كَفَّيْهِ.

٤٥. فَإِنْ ضَرَبَ مَرَّتَيْنِ فَلَا بَأْسَ.

Allāh ﷻ says: "*...and do not find water, then seek clean earth and wipe over your faces and hands with it. Allāh does not intend to make difficulty for you, but he intends to purify you and complete His favour upon you that you may be grateful.*" (5:6)

It was reported on the authority of Jābir ؓ that the Prophet ﷺ said, "I have been given five things no other prophet before me was given: Allāh ﷻ made me victorious by awe (of frightening my enemies) for a distance of one month's journey. The earth has been made for me a place of praying and purification. Therefore, one should pray whenever the time of prayer comes. War booty has been made halal for me, which was not allowed for anyone before me. I have been given the *shafāʿah* (intercession). Each prophet was sent to his nation specifically whereas I have been sent to the whole of mankind." (Agreed upon)

46. The following are not allowed for someone in a state of *ḥadath aṣghar* (minor state of ritual impurity):

1. To pray.
2. Circumambulation (*ṭawāf*) of the *Kaʿbah.*
3. To touch the Qurʾān.

قَالَ اللَّهُ تَعَالَى: ﴿فَلَمْ تَجِدُواْ مَآءً فَتَيَمَّمُواْ صَعِيدًا طَيِّبًا فَٱمْسَحُواْ بِوُجُوهِكُمْ وَأَيْدِيكُم مِّنْهُۚ مَا يُرِيدُ ٱللَّهُ لِيَجْعَلَ عَلَيْكُم مِّنْ حَرَجٍ وَلَٰكِن يُرِيدُ لِيُطَهِّرَكُمْ وَلِيُتِمَّ نِعْمَتَهُۥ عَلَيْكُمْ لَعَلَّكُمْ تَشْكُرُونَ ۝٦﴾ [المائِد: ٦]

وَعَنْ جَابِرٍ أَنَّ النَّبِيَّ صَلَّى اللهُ عَلَيْهِ وسلَّم قَالَ: «أُعْطِيتُ خَمْسًا لَمْ يُعْطَهُنَّ أَحَدٌ مِنْ الأَنْبِيَاءِ قَبْلِي: نُصِرْتُ بِالرُّعْبِ مَسِيرَةَ شَهْرٍ، وَجُعِلَتْ لِيَ الأَرْضُ مَسْجِدًا وَطَهُورًا، فَأَيَّمَا رَجُلٌ أَدْرَكَتْهُ الصَّلَاةُ فَلْيُصَلِّ، وَأُحِلَّتْ لِيَ الغَنَائِمُ، وَلَمْ تَحِلَّ لِأَحَدٍ قَبْلِي، وَأُعْطِيتُ الشَّفَاعَةَ، وَكَانَ النَّبِيُّ يُبْعَثُ إِلَى قَوْمِهِ خَاصَّةً، وَبُعِثْتُ إِلَى النَّاسِ عَامَّةً.» مُتَّفَقٌ عَلَيْهِ

٤٦. وَمَنْ عَلَيْهِ حَدَثٌ أَصْغَرُ لَمْ يَحِلَّ لَهُ

١. أَنْ يُصَلِّيَ

٢. ولا أَنْ يَطُوفَ بِالبَيْتِ

٣. وَلا يَمَسَّ الْمُصْحَفَ

The following are *also* not allowed if one is in a state of *ḥadath akbar* (major state of ritual impurity):

1. To recite anything from the Qurʾān.
2. To stay in a mosque without being in a state of *wuḍūʾ*.

The following are *also* not allowed for the woman who is menstruating or has post-natal bleeding:

1. To fast.
2. To have sexual intercourse with her.
3. To divorce her.

٤٧. وَيَزِيدُ مَنْ عَلَيْهِ حَدَثٌ أَكْبَرُ:

١. أَنَّهُ لا يَقْرَأُ شَيْئًا مِنَ القُرْآنِ

٢.وَلا يَلْبَثُ فِي الْمَسْجِدِ بِلا وُضُوءٍ

٤٨. وَتَزِيدُ الحَائِضُ والنُّفَسَاءُ

١. أَنَّهَا لا تَصُومُ

٢. وَلا يَحِلُّ وَطْؤُهَا

٣. وَلا طَلَاقُهَا

بَابُ الحَيْضِ

Chapter: Menstruation

49. Blood that is discharged from a woman's private part should at first be considered to be menstrual blood, regardless of age, amount of blood or repetition.

50. Except if the blood continuously flows and does not stop except for a short while. In that case she will be considered to be *mustaḥāḍah* (i.e. suffering from defective bleeding).

51. The Prophet ﷺ commanded the *mustaḥāḍah* to observe the rulings of menstruation according to the duration of her usual cycle.

52. If she doesn't have a regular cycle (*ʿādah*), then she has to try and distinguish between the blood of menstruation and the blood that results from a defective condition.

53. If she is unable to distinguish between the types of blood, she should then consider her menstruation to be six or seven days, as that is the average for each woman.

And Allāh ﷻ knows best.

بَابُ الحَيْضِ

٤٩. وَالْأَصْلُ فِي الدَّمِ الذِي يُصِيبُ المرْأَةَ أَنَّهُ حَيْضٌ، بِلَا حَدٍّ لِسِنِّهِ، وَلَا قَدْرِهِ، وَلَا تَكَرُّرِهِ.

٥٠. إِلَّا إِنْ أَطْبَقَ الدَّمُ عَلَى المرْأَةِ، أَوْ صَارَ لَا يَنْقَطِعُ عَنْهَا إِلَّا يَسِيرًا، فَإِنَّهَا تَصِيرُ مُسْتَحَاضَةً.

٥١. فَقَدْ أَمَرَهَا النَّبِيُّ ﷺ أَنْ تَجْلِسَ عَادَتَهَا.

٥٢. فَإِنْ لَمْ يَكُنْ لَهَا عَادَةٌ، فَإِلَى تَمْيِيزِهَا.

٥٣. فَإِنْ لَمْ يَكُنْ لَهَا تَمْيِيزٌ، فَإِلَى عَادَةِ النِّسَاءِ الغَالِبَةِ: سِتَّةِ أَيَّامٍ أَوْ سَبْعَةٍ

وَاللَّهُ أَعْلَمُ.

كِتَابُ الصَّلاة

(شُرُوطُ الصَّلاة)

The Book of Prayer
(Conditions of Prayer)

It has already preceded that purification is from the conditions of prayer.

54. Another condition is that the time for prayer must have entered.

55. The basis of this condition is based on the narration of Jibrīl, "...that he led the Prophet ﷺ (in prayer) at the earliest and latest time (of the prayer) and said, "O Muḥammad ﷺ, the prayer is to be performed between these two times." (Aḥmad, Nasāʾi and Tirmidhi)

56. It was reported on the authority of ʿAbdullāh ibn ʿAmr ﷺ that the Prophet ﷺ said,

"The time of *Ẓuhr* is when the sun passes the meridian (until) a man's shadow is of the same length as his height. It lasts until the time of ʿ*Aṣr*.

The time of ʿ*Aṣr* is as long as the sun has not become yellow (during its setting).

كِتَابُ الصَّلَاةِ

(شُرُوطُ الصَّلَاةِ)

تَقَدَّمَ أَنَّ الطَّهَارَةَ مِنْ شُرُوطِهَا:

٥٤. وَمِنْ شُرُوطِهَا: دُخُولُ الوَقْتِ.

٥٥. وَالْأَصْلُ فِيهِ حَدِيثُ جِبْرِيلَ: أَنَّهُ أَمَّ النَّبِيَّ ﷺ فِي أَوَّلِ الوَقْتِ وَآخِرِهِ، وَقَالَ: «يَا مُحَمَّدُ، الصَّلَاةُ مَا بَيْنَ هَذَيْنِ الوَقْتَيْنِ.» رَوَاهُ أَحْمَدُ وَالنَّسَائِيُّ وَالتِّرْمِذِيُّ.

٥٦. وَعَنْ عَبْدِ اللَّهِ بْنِ عَمْرو رَضِيَ اللَّهُ عَنْهُمَا أَنَّ النَّبِيَّ ﷺ قَالَ:

«وَقْتُ الظُّهْرِ: إِذَا زَالَتِ الشَّمْسُ، وَكَانَ ظِلُّ الرَّجُلِ كَطُولِهِ، مَا لَمْ تَحْضُرِ العَصْرُ،

وَوَقْتُ العَصْرِ: مَا لَمْ تَصْفَرَّ الشَّمْسُ،

The time of *Maghrib* is as long as the twilight has not disappeared.

The time of *ʿIshāʾ* is up to midnight.

And the time of *Fajr* is from the appearance of dawn as long as the sun has not risen." (Muslim)

57. The prayer is caught within the time of prayer if one *rakʿah* (unit) was performed due to the statement of the Prophet ﷺ, "Whoever caught one *rakʿah* from the prayer has caught the whole prayer." (Agreed upon)

58. It is not permissible to delay it, or to delay part of it from its stated time due to any reason.

59. Except if one delayed it in order to combine it with another prayer, which is allowed due to travelling, rain and illness etc.

60. It is more virtuous to perform the prayer in its earliest time except for:

1. *ʿIshāʾ*, if it is not too difficult upon the worshippers.
2. *Ẓuhr*, when the weather is extremely hot.

وَوَقْتُ صَلَاةِ المغْرِبِ: مَا لَمْ يَغِبِ الشَّفَقُ،

وَوَقْتُ صَلَاةِ العِشَاءِ: إِلَى نِصْفِ اللَّيْلِ.» رَوَاهُ مُسْلِمٌ.

٥٧. وَيُدْرَكُ وَقْتُ الصَّلَاةِ بِإِدْرَاكِ رَكْعَةٍ ؛ لِقَوْلِهِ ﷺ: «مَنْ أَدْرَكَ رَكْعَةً مِنَ الصَّلَاةِ، فَقَدْ أَدْرَكَ الصَّلَاةَ.» مُتَّفَقٌ عَلَيْهِ.

٥٨. وَلَا يَحِلُّ تَأْخِيرُهَا، أَوْ تَأْخِيرُ بَعْضِهَا عَنْ وَقْتِهَا لِعُذْرٍ أَوْ غَيْرِهِ.

٥٩. إِلَّا إِذَا أَخَّرَهَا لِيَجْمَعَهَا مَعَ غَيْرِهَا، فَإِنَّهُ يَجُوزُ لِعُذْرٍ مِنْ: سَفَرٍ، أَوْ مَطَرٍ أَوْ مَرَضٍ، أَوْ نَحْوِهَا.

٦٠. وَالْأَفْضَلُ تَقْدِيمُ الصَّلَاةِ فِي أَوَّلِ وَقْتِهَا إِلَّا:

١. العِشَاءَ إِذَا لَمْ يُشَقَّ.

٢. الظُّهرَ في شِدَّةِ الحَرِّ

The Prophet ﷺ said, "When it is very hot, delay the prayer (*Ẓuhr*) until it cools down, for the intensity of the heat is from the exhalation of Hell." (Agreed upon)

61. If one missed a prayer it is obligatory to make it up immediately and in order.

62. If one forgot the order or was ignorant of it or feared the exiting of the time for the current prayer; then the (obligation of) order falls between the missed prayer and the current prayer.

63. From the conditions of the prayer: covering the *ʿawrah* (nakedness) with permissible, non-transparent clothing.

64. There are three types of *ʿawrah:*

1. *Mughallaẓah* (major)*:* This is the *ʿawrah* of a mature free female. All of her body is *ʿawrah* apart from her face.

2. *Mukhaffafah* (light)*:* This is the *ʿawrah* of a child between the ages of seven up to ten. The *ʿawrah* for them is to cover the two private parts.

3. *Mutawassiṭah* (medium)*:* This is the *ʿawrah* of everyone else not mentioned above. The *ʿawrah* for them is from the navel to the knees.

قَالَ النَّبِيُّ صلى الله عليه وسلم: «إِذَا اشْتَدَّ الْحَرُّ فَأَبْرِدُوا عَنِ الصَّلاةِ، فَإِنَّ شِدَّةَ الْحَرِّ مِنْ فَيْحِ جَهَنَّم.»

٦١. وَمَنْ فَاتَتْهُ صَلَاةٌ وَجَبَ عَلَيْهِ قَضَاؤُهَا فَوْرًا مُرَتَّبًا.

٦٢. فَإِنْ نَسِيَ التَّرْتِيبَ أَوْ جَهِلَهُ، أَوْ خَافَ فَوْتَ الصَّلَاةِ، سَقَطَ التَّرْتِيبُ بَيْنَهَا وَبَيْنَ الحَاضِرَةِ.

٦٣. وَمِنْ شُرُوطِهَا سَتْرُ العَوْرَةِ بِثَوْبٍ مُبَاحٍ لَا يَصِفُ البَشْرَةَ.

٦٤. وَالْعَوْرَةُ ثَلَاثَةُ أَنْوَاعٍ:

١. مُغَلَّظَةٌ، وَهِيَ: عَوْرَةُ المَرْأَةِ الحُرَّةِ البَالِغَةِ، فَجَمِيعُ بَدَنِهَا عَوْرَةٌ فِي الصَّلَاةِ إِلَّا وَجْهَهَا.

٢. مُخَفَّفَةٌ، وهي: عَوْرَةُ اِبْنِ سَبْعِ سِنِينَ إِلَى عَشْرٍ، وَهِيَ الفَرْجَانِ.

٣. وَمُتَوَسِّطَةٌ، وَهِيَ: عَوْرَةُ مَنْ عَدَاهُمْ، مِنَ السُّرَّةِ إِلَى الرُّكْبَةِ

*Allāh ﷻ says in the Qurʾān, *"O Children of Ādam, take your adornment at every place of prayer..."* (7: 31)

65. From the conditions: facing the *qiblah.*

Allāh ﷻ says in the Qurʾān, *"So from wherever you go out, turn your face toward al Masjid al Ḥarām..."* (2: 149)

66. If one was unable to face the *qiblah* due to an illness or any other (valid) reason, the condition to face the *qiblah* will be dropped. Similarly, all obligations drop when one is incapable of doing them.

Allāh ﷻ says, *"And fear Allāh as much as you all can..."* (64: 16)

67. The Prophet ﷺ used to pray *nāfilah* (recommended) prayers on his riding animal in whatever direction it turned to. (Agreed upon) Moreover, in another narration it states that he did not pray the obligatory prayers on it.

68. From the conditions (of prayer): the intention.

قَالَ تَعَالَى: ﴿يَٰبَنِيٓ ءَادَمَ خُذُواْ زِينَتَكُمۡ عِندَ كُلِّ مَسۡجِدٖ﴾ [الأعراف: ٣١]

٦٥. وَمِنْهَا: اِسْتِقْبَالُ القِبْلَةِ:

قَالَ تَعَالَى: ﴿وَمِنۡ حَيۡثُ خَرَجۡتَ فَوَلِّ وَجۡهَكَ شَطۡرَ ٱلۡمَسۡجِدِ ٱلۡحَرَامِۚ﴾ [البقرة: ١٤٩]

٦٦. فَإِنْ عَجَزَ عَنْ اِسْتِقْبَالِهَا، لِمَرَضٍ أَوْ غَيْرِهِ سَقَطَ، كَمَا تَسْقُطُ جَمِيعُ الوَاجِبَاتِ بِالْعَجْزِ عَنْهَا.

قَالَ تَعَالَى: ﴿فَٱتَّقُواْ ٱللَّهَ مَا ٱسۡتَطَعۡتُمۡ﴾ [التغابن: ١٦]

٦٧. وَكَانَ النَّبِي صَلَّى اللهُ عَلَيْهِ وَسَلَّمَ يُصَلِّي فِي السَّفَرِ النَّافِلَةَ عَلَى رَاحِلَتِهِ حَيْثُ تَوَجَّهتْ بِهِ. مُتَّفَقٌ عَلَيْهِ. وَفِي لَفْظٍ: غَيْرَ أَنَّهُ لَا يُصَلِّي المكْتُوبَةَ.

٦٨. وَمِنْ شُرُوطِهَا: النِّيَّةُ

69. It is permissible to perform the prayer in every location apart from:

1. An impure place.
2. On usurped land.
3. A graveyard.
4. A *ḥammām* (public bath)
5. A camel's stable.

The Prophet ﷺ said in an authentic narration found in Tirmidhi, "All of the earth is a *masjid* except the graveyard and *ḥammām*."

٦٩. وَتَصِحُّ الصَّلَاةُ فِي كُلِّ مَوْضِعٍ إِلَّا:

١. فِي مَحَلٍّ نَجِسٍ.

٢. أَوْ مَغْصُوبٍ.

٣. أَوْ فِي مَقْبَرَةٍ.

٤. أَوْ حَمَّامٍ.

٥. أَوْ أَعْطَانِ إِبِلٍ.

وَفِي سُنَنِ التِّرْمِذِيِّ مَرْفُوعًا «الأَرْضُ كُلُّهَا مَسْجِدٌ، إِلَّا المقْبَرَةَ وَالْحَمَّامَ.»

بَابُ صِفَةِ الصَّلاة

Chapter: The Description of Prayer

70. It is recommended to approach the prayer with tranquillity and dignity.

71. When one enters the mosque they should say:

بِسْمِ اللهِ، والصَّلاةُ والسَّلامُ عَلَى رَسُولِ اللهِ، اللَّهُمَّ اغْفِرْ لِي ذُنُوبِي وَافْتَحْ لِي أَبْوَابَ رَحْمَتِكَ

Bismillāh waṣ-ṣalātu was-salāmu ʿalā Rasūlillāh. Allāhummagh-firli dhunūbi waf-taḥ li abwāba raḥmatik

"In the name of Allāh and may the peace and blessings be upon the Messenger of Allāh, O Allāh forgive my sins and open for me your doors of mercy." (Ibn Mājah)

72. One should enter the mosque with the right foot.

73. And leave the mosque with the left foot.

بَابُ صِفَةِ الصَّلَاةِ

٧٠. يُسْتَحَبُّ أَنْ يَأْتِيَ إِلَيْهَا بِسَكِينَةٍ وَوَقَارٍ.

٧١. فَإِذَا دَخَلَ المسْجِدَ قَالَ: «بِاسْمِ اللَّهِ، وَالصَّلَاةُ وَالسَّلَامُ عَلَى رَسُولِ اللَّهِ، اللَّهُمَّ اغْفِرْ لِي ذُنُوبِي وَافْتَحْ لِي أَبْوَابَ رَحْمَتِكَ.»

٧٢. وَيُقَدِّمُ رِجْلَهُ اليُمْنَى لِدُخُولِ المسْجِدِ

٧٣. واليُسْرَى لِلْخُرُوجِ مِنْهُ

74. One should mention the same duʿāʾ when leaving but replace the ending with:

وَافْتَحْ لِي أَبْوَابَ فَضْلِكَ

Waf-taḥ li abwāba faḍlik
"...and open for me your doors of graciousness." (Aḥmad and Ibn Mājah)

75. One begins the prayer by saying, "*Allāhu Akbar*".

76. One should raise their hands parallel to their shoulders or their earlobes in four places:

1. With the opening *takbir.*
2. When descending into the bowing position (*rukūʿ.*)
3. When rising from it.
4. When one has stood up from the first *tashahhud* as has been authentically reported from the Prophet.

77. One should place the right hand upon the left hand,

78. above the navel, under it or upon the chest.

٧٤. وَيُقُولُ هَذَا الذِّكْرَ، إلا أَنَّهُ يَقُولُ: وَافْتَحْ لِي أَبْوَابَ فَضْلِكَ، كَمَا وَرَدَ فِي ذلك الحَدِيثِ الذِي رَوَاهُ أَحْمَدُ وَابْنُ مَاجه.

٧٥. فَإِذَا قَامَ إِلَى الصَّلَاةِ قَالَ: «اللَّهُ أَكْبَرُ».

٧٦. وَيَرْفَعُ يَدَيْهِ إِلَى حَذْوِ مَنْكِبَيْهِ، أَوْ إِلَى شَحْمَةِ أُذُنَيْهِ، فِي أَرْبَعَةِ مَوَاضِعَ:

١. عِنْدَ تَكْبِيرَةِ الإِحْرَامِ.

٢. وَعِنْدَ الرُّكُوعِ.

٣. وَعِنْدَ الرَّفْعِ مِنْهُ، وَعِنْدَ القِيَامِ مِن التَّشَهُّدِ الأَوَّلِ، كَمَا صَحَّتْ بِذَلِكَ الأَحَادِيثُ عَنْ النَّبِي صَلَّى اللهُ عَلَيْهِ وَسَلَّمَ.

٧٧. وَيَضَعُ يَدَهُ اليُمْنَى عَلَى اليُسْرَى.

٧٨. فَوْقَ سُرَّتِهِ، أَوْ تَحْتَهَا، أَوْ عَلَى صَدْرِهِ.

79. Then one should say:

سُبْحَانَكَ اللَّهُمَّ وَبِحَمْدِكَ، وَتَبَارَكَ اسْمُكَ، وتَعَالى جَدُّكَ، وَلا إلَهَ غَيْرُكَ

Subḥanaka Allāhumma wa bi-ḥamdika wa tabārakas-muka wa taʿāla jadduka wa lā ilāha ghayruka

"Glory and praise be to You, O Allāh. Blessed be Your name and exalted be Your majesty, there is none worthy of worship except You."

One can say any other opening supplication that has been reported from the Prophet.

80. Then one should seek refuge in Allāh ﷻ.

81. Then say the *basmalah.*
82. Then read opening chapter of the Qurʾān, *al Fātiḥah.*

83. One should read after the *Fātiḥah* another chapter in the first two units of a three and four-unit prayer. These chapters being:

1. From the long *mufaṣṣal* chapters for *Fajr.*
2. From the short *mufaṣṣal* chapters for *Maghrib.*
3. From average length *mufaṣṣal* chapters for the rest of the prayers.

٧٩. وَيَقُولُ: سُبْحَانَكَ اللَّهُمَّ وَبِحَمْدِكَ، وَتَبَارَكَ اسْمُكَ، وَتَعَالَى جَدُّكَ، وَلَا إِلَهَ غَيْرُكَ أَوْ غَيْرُهُ مِنْ الِاسْتِفْتَاحَاتِ الوَارِدَةِ عَنْ النَّبِيِّ ﷺ.

٨٠. ثُمَّ يَتَعَوَّذُ.

٨١. وَيُبَسْمِلُ.

٨٢. وَيَقْرَأُ الفَاتِحَةَ.

٨٣. وَيَقْرَأُ مَعَهَا، فِي الرَّكْعَتَيْنِ الأُولَيَيْنِ مِنْ الرُّبَاعِيَّةِ وَالثُّلَاثِيَّةِ سُورَةً تَكُونُ:

أ- فِي الفَجْرِ: مِنْ طِوَالِ المُفَصَّلِ.

ب - وفِي المَغْرِبِ: مِنْ قِصَارِهِ،

جـ - وفِي البَاقِي: مِنْ أَوْسَاطِهِ

84. One should recite aloud in the prayers that occur after sunset.

85. Whereas one should recite quietly in the daytime prayers, except for *Jumu'ah, ʿĪd, kusūf* (eclipse), and *istisqāʾ* (prayer asking for rain) prayers since they are to be prayed aloud.

86. Then one should say the *takbīr* for *rukūʿ*.

87. Then place one's hands upon their knees.

88. One's head should be parallel to their back.

89. One should then say:

سُبْحَانَ رَبِّيَ الْعَظِيم

Subḥāna Rabbil ʿAẓīm

"Glory be to my Lord, the All-Great."

and repeat it.

٨٤. يَجْهَرُ فِي القِرَاءَةِ لَيلًا.

٨٥. ويُسِرُّ بِهَا نَهَارًا، إِلَّا الجُمْعَةَ وَالْعِيدَ وَالْكُسُوفَ وَالِاسْتِسْقَاءَ، فَإِنَّهُ يَجْهَرُ بِهَا.

٨٦. ثُمَّ يُكَبِّرُ لِلرُّكُوعِ.

٨٧. وَيَضَعُ يَدَيْهِ عَلَى رُكْبَتَيْهِ.

٨٨. وَيَجْعَلُ رَأْسَهُ حِيَالَ ظَهْرِهِ.

٨٩. وَيَقُولُ: سُبْحَانَ رَبِّيَ العَظِيمِ. وَيُكَرِّرُهُ.

90. One can also say in their *rukūʿ* or *sujūd:*

سُبْحَانَكَ اللَّهُمَّ رَبَّنَا وَبِحَمْدِكَ، اللَّهُمَّ اغْفِرْ لِي

Subḥanaka Allāhumma Rabbana wa biḥamdika Allāhumma ighfir lī

"Glory be to You O Allāh, Our Lord, and praise. O Allāh, forgive me."

91. Then one should raise their head

92. saying,

سَمِعَ اللهُ لِمَنْ حَمِدَهُ

Samiʿallāhu liman ḥamidah

"Allāh hears those who praise Him."

whether one is an Imām or *Munfarid.* (someone who prays alone).

٩٠. وَإِنْ قَالَ مَعَ ذَلِكَ حَالَ رُكُوعِهِ وَسُجُودِهِ: «سُبْحَانَكَ اللَّهُمَّ رَبَّنَا وَبِحَمْدِكَ، اللَّهُمَّ اغْفِرْ لِي.» فَحَسَنٌ.

٩١. ثُم يَرْفَعُ رَأْسَهُ.

٩٢. قَائِلًا سَمِعَ اللهُ لِمَنْ حَمِدَهُ، إِن كَانَ إِمَامًا أَوْ مُنْفَرِدًا.

93. Then everyone should say:

رَبَّنَا ولَكَ الحَمْد، حَمْداً كَثِيراً طَيِّباً مُبَارَكاً فِيهِ مِلْءَ السَّمَاء، ومِلْءَ الأَرْضِ وَمِلْءَ مَا شِئْتَ مِنْ شَيْءٍ بَعْدُ

Rabbanā wa lakal ḥamd, ḥamdan kathīran ṭayyiban mubārakan fīh, milʾas-samāʾ wa milʾal arḍi wa milʾa mā shiʾta min shayʾin baʿd

"Our Lord, and to You be all praise, so much pure praise, inherently blessed, filling the sky, the earth, and filling whatever else you wish."

94. Then one should prostrate on their "seven limbs" as the Prophet ﷺ said, "I have been ordered to prostrate upon seven bones; the forehead – He then pointed to his nose – and the hands, the knees and the toes." (Agreed upon)

95. One should then say:

سُبْحَانَ رَبِّيَ الأَعْلَى

Subḥāna Rabbi al-Aʿlā

"Glory be to my Lord, the All-High"

96. Then pronounce the *takbīr.*

٩٣. وَيَقُولُ الكُلُّ رَبَّنَا وَلَكَ الحَمْدُ، حَمْدًا كَثِيرًا طَيِّبًا مُبَارَكًا فِيهِ، مِلْءَ السَّمَاءِ، وَمِلْءَ الأَرْضِ، وَمِلْءَ مَا شِئْتَ مِنْ شَيْءٍ بَعْدُ.

٩٤. ثُمَّ يَسْجُدُ عَلَى أَعْضَائِهِ السَّبْعَةِ: كَمَا قَالَ النَّبِيُّ ﷺ «أُمِرْتُ أَنْ أَسْجُدَ عَلَى سَبْعَةِ أَعْظُمٍ: عَلَى الجَبْهَةِ – وَأَشَارَ بِيَدِهِ إِلَى أَنْفِهِ – وَالْكَفَّيْنِ، وَالرُّكْبَتَيْنِ، وَأَطْرَافِ القَدَمَيْنِ.» مُتَّفَقٌ عَلَيْه.

٩٥. وَيَقُولُ: «سُبْحَانَ رَبِّيَ الأَعْلَى.»

٩٦. ثُمَّ يُكَبِّرُ.

97. Then one should sit on their left foot and erect their right foot. This position is called *iftirāsh.*

98. One should sit in that position in all his sittings except in the last *tashahhud* whereby he should sit in the *tawarruk* position, which is to sit on the floor (i.e. to have the buttocks on the floor) and to put the left foot under his right thigh and shin.

99. Then one should say (after rising from the first prostration):

رَبِّ اغْفِرْ لِي، وَارْحَمْنِي، وَاهْدِنِي، وَارْزُقْنِي، واجْبُرْنِي وَعَافِنِي

Rabbighfir lī war-ḥamni, wah-dini, war-zuqni wajburni wa ʿāfinī

"O my Lord! Forgive me, have mercy on me, guide me, sustain me, strengthen me and protect me."

100. Then one should prostrate like they did for the first prostration.

101. Then one should rise whilst saying the *takbīr,* depending on the soles of their feet.

102. Then one should pray the next *rakʿah* (unit) as they prayed the first one.

٩٧. وَيَجْلِسُ عَلَى رِجْلِهِ الْيُسْرَى، وَيَنْصِبُ الْيُمْنَى وَهُوَ الِافْتِرَاشُ.

٩٨. وَيَفْعَلُ ذَلِكَ فِي جَمِيعِ جَلَسَاتِ الصَّلَاةِ إِلَّا فِي التَّشَهُّدِ الْأَخِيرِ فَإِنَّهُ يَتَوَرَّكُ: بِأَنْ يَجْلِسَ عَلَى الْأَرْضِ وَيُخْرِجُ رِجْلَهُ الْيُسْرَى مِنْ الْخَلْفِ الْأَيْمَنِ.

٩٩. وَيَقُولُ: «رَبِّ اغْفِرْ لِي، وَارْحَمْنِي، وَاهْدِنِي، وَارْزُقْنِي، وَاجْبُرْنِي وَعَافِنِي.»

١٠٠. ثُمَّ يَسْجُدُ الثَّانِيَةَ كَالْأُولَى.

١٠١. ثُمَّ يَنْهَضُ مُكَبِّرًا، عَلَى صُدُورِ قَدَمَيْهِ.

١٠٢. وَيُصَلِّي الرَّكْعَةَ الثَّانِيَةَ كَالْأُولَى.

103. Then one should sit for the first *tashahhud.*

104. The following is the supplication for the *tashahhud:*

التَّحِيَّاتُ لِلهِ، وَالصَّلَوَاتُ، وَالطَّيِّبَاتُ، السَّلامُ عَلَيْكَ أَيُّهَا النَّبِيُّ وَرَحْمَةُ اللهِ وَبَرَكَاتُهُ، السَّلامُ عَلَيْنَا وَعَلَى عِبَادِ اللهِ الصَّالِحِين، أَشْهَدُ أَنْ لا الهَ الا الله، وَأَشْهَدُ أَنَّ مُحَمَّداً عَبْدُهُ وَرَسُولُهُ

At-Taḥiyyātu lillāhi waṣ-ṣalawātu waṭ-ṭayyibāt, as-Salāmu ʿalayka ayyuhan-Nabiyyu wa raḥmatullāhi wa barakātuh, as-Salāmu ʿalaynā wa ʿalā ʿibādillahiṣ-ṣāliḥīn, ash-hadu an lā ilāha illallāhu wa ash-hadu anna Muḥammadan ʿabduhu wa Rasūluh

"All compliments, prayers and pure words are due to Allāh, Peace be upon you, O Prophet, and also the mercy of Allāh and His blessings. Peace be upon us, and on the righteous slaves of Allāh. I bear witness that none has the right to be worshipped except Allāh, and I bear witness that Muḥammad is His slave and messenger."

105. Then one should say the *takbīr* (and rise).

106. One should then pray the rest of the prayer reciting only *al Fātiḥah* for each *rakʿah.*

107. Then he should say the last *tashahhud* (whilst seated), as stated above.

١٠٣. ثُمَّ يَجْلِسُ لِلتَّشَهُّدِ الأَوَّلِ.

١٠٤. وَصِفَتُهُ: «التَّحِيَّاتُ لِلَّهِ، وَالصَّلَوَاتُ، وَالطَّيِّبَاتُ، السَّلَام عَلَيْك أَيُّهَا النَّبِيُّ وَرَحْمَةُ اللَّهِ وَبَرَكَاتُهُ، السَّلَامُ عَلَيْنَا وَعَلَى عِبَادِ اللَّهِ الصَّالِحِينَ، أَشْهَدُ أَنْ لَا إِلَهَ إِلَّا اللَّهُ، وَأَشْهَدُ أَنَّ مُحَمَّدًا عَبْدُهُ وَرَسُولُهُ.»

١٠٥. ثُمَّ يُكَبِّرُ.

١٠٦. وَيُصَلِّي بَاقِي صَلَاتِهِ بِالْفَاتِحَةِ فِي كُلِّ رَكْعَةٍ.

١٠٧. ثُمَّ يَتَشَهَّدُ التَّشَهُّدَ الأَخِيرَ وَهُوَ المذْكُورُ

108. However, one should add the following:

اللَّهُمَّ صَلِّ عَلَى مُحَمَّدٍ وَعَلَى آلِ مُحَمَّدٍ، كَمَا صَلَّيْتَ عَلَى آلِ إِبْرَاهِيمَ إِنَّكَ حَمِيدٌ مَجِيدٌ، وَبَارِكْ عَلَى مُحَمَّدٍ وَعَلَى آلِ مُحَمَّدٍ، كَمَا بَارَكْتَ عَلَى آلِ إِبْرَاهِيمَ، إِنَّكَ حَمِيدٌ مَجِيد

Allāhumma ṣalli ʿalā Muḥammadin wa ʿalā āli Muḥammadin kamā ṣallayta ʿalā āli Ibrāhīma innaka Ḥamīdun Majīd wa bārik ʿalā Muḥammadin wa ʿalā āli Muḥammadin kamā bārakta ʿalā āli Ibrāhīma, innaka Ḥamīdun Majīd

"O Allāh! Send prayers upon Muḥammad, and on the family of Muḥammad, as you sent prayers on the family Ibrāhīm; you are indeed worthy of praise, full of glory. And send blessings upon Muḥammad, and on the family of Muḥammad, as you sent blessings on the family of Ibrāhīm; you are indeed worthy of praise, full of glory."

أَعُوذُ بِاللهِ مِنْ عَذَابِ جَهَنَّمَ، وَمِنْ عَذَابِ القَبْرِ، وَمِنْ فِتْنَةِ المَحْيَا وَالمَمَاتِ، وَمِنْ فِتْنَةِ المَسِيحِ الدَّجَّالِ

Aʿūdhu billāhi min ʿathābi Jahannam wa min ʿathābil qabri wa min fitnatil maḥyā wal mamāt wa min fitnatil masīḥid-dajjāl

"O Allāh! I seek refuge in you from the punishment of the fire, from the punishment of the grave, from the trial of life and death, and from the trial of the anti-Christ."

One may also make other supplications.

١٠٨. وَيَزِيدُ عَلَى مَا تَقَدَّمَ:

١. اللَّهُمَّ صَلِّ عَلَى مُحَمَّدٍ وَعَلَى آلِ مُحَمَّدٍ، كَمَا صَلَّيْتَ عَلَى آلِ إِبْرَاهِيمَ إِنَّكَ حَمِيدٌ مَجِيدٌ، وَبَارِكْ عَلَى مُحَمَّدٍ وَعَلَى آلِ مُحَمَّدٍ، كَمَا بَارَكْتَ عَلَى آلِ إِبْرَاهِيمَ، إِنَّكَ حَمِيدٌ مَجِيدٌ.

٢. أَعُوذُ بِاللَّهِ مِنْ عَذَابِ جَهَنَّمَ، وَمِنْ عَذَابِ الْقَبْرِ، وَمِنْ فِتْنَةِ الْمَحْيَا وَالْمَمَاتِ، وَمِنْ فِتْنَةِ الْمَسِيحِ الدَّجَّالِ.

٣. وَيَدْعُو اللَّهَ بِمَا أَحَبَّ.

109. Then one should do the *taslīm* (salutations) to their right and (then) their left, according to the narration of Wāʾil ibn Ḥujr which was reported by Abū Dāwūd:

السَّلَامُ عَلَيْكُمْ وَرَحْمَةُ اللهِ

As-Salāmu ʿalaykum wa raḥmatullāh

"May the peace and mercy of Allāh be upon you."

110. The verbal pillars (*arkān qawliyyah*) for the prayer are:

1. The opening *takbīr.*
2. The recitation of the *Fātiḥah* other than the *maʾmūm* (follower).
3. The last *tashahhud.*
4. The *taslīm.*

111. The rest of the actions in prayer are from the physical pillars (*arkān fiʿliyyah)* except for:

1. The first *tashahhud,* since it is from the *wājibāt* (obligations) of the prayer.
2. The *takbīrs* apart from the opening *takbīr.*
3. Saying *subḥāna rabbi al-ʿaẓīm* in *rukūʿ*
4. Saying *subḥāna rabbi al-aʿlā* in *sujūd.*
5. Saying *rabbigh-firli* between the two prostrations at least once. To increase the times one says it is recommended.

١٠٩. ثُمَّ يُسَلِّمُ عَنْ يَمِينِهِ، وَعَنْ يَسَارِهِ «السَّلَامُ عَلَيْكُمْ وَرَحْمَةُ اللَّهِ.» لِحَدِيثِ وَائِلِ بْنِ حُجْرٍ، رَوَاهُ أَبُو دَاوُدَ.

١١٠. وَالْأَرْكَانُ القَوْلِيَّةُ مِنْ المذْكُورَاتِ:

١. تَكْبِيرَةُ الإِحْرَامِ.

٢. وَقِرَاءَةُ الفَاتِحَةِ عَلَى غَيْرِ مَأْمُومٍ.

٣. وَالتَّشَهُّدُ الأَخِيرُ.

٤. وَالسَّلَامُ.

١١١. وَبَاقِي أَفْعَالِهَا: أَرْكَانٌ فِعْلِيَّةٌ، إِلَّا:

١. التَّشَهُّدَ الأَوَّلَ، فَإِنَّهُ مِنْ وَاجِبَاتِ الصَّلَاةِ.

٢. وَالتَّكْبِيرَاتِ غَيْرَ تَكْبِيرَةِ الإِحْرَامِ.

٣. وقولَ «سُبْحَانَ رَبِّيَ العَظِيم.» في الرُّكُوع

٤. و«سُبْحَانَ رَبِّيَ الأَعْلَى» مَرَّةً فِي السُّجُودِ.

٥. و«رَبِّ اِغْفِرْ لِي» بَيْنَ السَّجْدَتَيْنِ مَرَّةً، مَرَّةً، وَمَا زَادَ فَهُوَ مَسْنُونٌ.

6. Saying *samiʿallāhu liman ḥamidah* for the Imām and *munfarid.*
7. Saying *rabbanā lakal ḥamd* for everyone.

112. These (aforementioned) obligations (*wājibāt*) do not have to be made up if one forgot to do them. However, one has to perform the Prostration of Forgetfulness (*sujūd al sahw*) to make up for the missed obligations.

113. The pillars (*arkān*) cannot be dropped due to forgetfulness, ignorance or if missed intentionally.

114. The rest of the actions and statements in the prayer are recommended and perfect the prayer.

115. Having *ṭumaʾnīnah* (to have peace/tranquillity [i.e. for the bones to be at ease]) is from the pillars (*arkān*) of the prayer.

Abū Hurayrah ﷺ narrated that the Prophet ﷺ said, "If you are ready for prayer, perform your ablution well, then face the *qiblah* and say the *takbīr.* Then read from what you know from the Qurʾān, then bow until you are at ease while bowing, then rise until you are upright, then prostrate until you are at ease while prostrating, then rise until you are at ease while sitting, then prostrate again until you are at ease while prostrating. Do that for the rest of your prayer." (Agreed upon)

٦. وَقَوْلَ: «سَمِعَ اللَّهُ لِمَنْ حَمِدَهُ» لِلْإِمَامِ وَالْمُنْفَرِدِ.

٧. و «رَبَّنَا لَكَ الحَمْدُ» لِلْكُلِّ.

١١٢. فَهَذِهِ الوَاجِبَاتُ تَسْقُطُ بِالسَّهْوِ، وَيَجْبُرُهَا سُجُودُهُ السَّهْوَ، وَكَذَا بِالْجَهْلِ.

١١٣. وَالْأَرْكَانُ لَا تَسْقُطُ سَهْوًا وَلَا جَهْلاً وَلَا عَمْدًا.

١١٤. وَالْبَاقِي سُنَنُ أَقْوَالٍ وَأَفْعَالٍ مُكْمِلٍ لِلصَّلَاةِ.

١١٥. وَمِنْ الأَرْكَانِ الطُّمَأْنِينَةُ فِي جَمِيعِ أَرْكَانِهَا.

وَعَنْ أَبِي هُرَيْرَةَ: أَنَّ النَّبِيَّ ﷺ قَالَ: «إِذَا قُمْتَ إِلَى الصَّلَاةِ فَأَسْبِغِ الوُضُوءَ، ثُمَّ اِسْتَقْبِلِ القِبْلَةَ فَكَبِّرْ، ثُمَّ اِقْرَأْ مَا تَيَسَّرَ مَعَكَ مِنْ القُرْآنِ، ثُمَّ اِرْكَعْ حَتَّى تَطْمَئِنَّ رَاكِعًا، ثُمَّ اِرْفَعْ حَتَّى تَعْتَدِلَ قَائِمًا، ثُمَّ اُسْجُدْ حَتَّى تَطْمَئِنَّ سَاجِدًا، ثُمَّ اِرْفَعْ حَتَّى تَطْمَئِنَّ جَالِسًا، ثُمَّ اُسْجُدْ حَتَّى تَطْمَئِنَّ سَاجِدًا ثُمَّ اِفْعَلْ ذَلِكَ فِي صَلَاتِكَ كُلِّهَا.» مُتَّفَقٌ عَلَيْهِ

The Prophet ﷺ also said, "Pray as you see me praying." (Agreed upon).

116. When one has finished from the prayer they should:

1. Seek Allāh's ﷻ forgiveness three times.

2. Say,

اللَّهُمَّ أَنْتَ السَّلامُ وَمِنْكَ السَّلامُ تَبارَكْتَ يَا ذَا الجَلالِ والإِكْرَام

Allāhumma anta as-Salām wa minkas-Salām, tabārakta yā dhal Jalāli wal Ikrām.

"O Allāh, You are the source of peace (or the One free from all faults) and from You comes peace, blessed are You, O Possessor of Majesty and Honour."

وَقَالَ ﷺ: «صَلُّوا كَمَا رَأَيْتُمُونِي أُصَلِّي.» مُتَّفَقٌ عَلَيْهِ.

١١٦. فَإِذَا فَرَغَ مِنْ صَلَاتِهِ:

١. اِسْتَغْفَرَ ثَلَاثًا، وَقَالَ:

٢. اللَّهُمَّ أَنْتَ السَّلَامُ وَمِنْكَ السَّلَامُ، تَبَارَكْتَ يَا ذَا الجَلَالِ وَالْإِكْرَامِ.

3.

لاَ إِلَهَ إِلاَّ اللَّهُ وَحْدَهُ لاَ شَرِيكَ لَهُ، لَهُ الْمُلْكُ وَلَهُ الْحَمْدُ وَهُوَ عَلَى كُلِّ شَيْءٍ قَدِيرٌ لاَ إِلَهَ إِلاَّ اللَّهُ وَلاَ نَعْبُدُ إِلاَّ إِيَّاهُ لَهُ النِّعْمَةُ وَلَهُ الْفَضْلُ وَلَهُ الثَّنَاءُ الْحَسَنُ لاَ إِلَهَ إِلاَّ اللَّهُ مُخْلِصِينَ لَهُ الدِّينَ وَلَوْ كَرِهَ الْكَافِرُونَ

Lā ilāha illal-lāh waḥdahu lā sharīka lah, lahul Mulk, wa lahul ḥamd, wa huwa ʿalā kulli shayʾin Qadīr. Lā ilāha illah-lāh, wa la naʿbudu illā iyyāh, lahun niʿmah, wa lahul faḍl, wa lahuth-thanāʾ al ḥasan, lā ilāha illal-lāh, mukhliṣīna lahud-dīna wa law karihal kāfirūn.

"There is no one worthy of worship except Allāh. He is alone. There is no partner with Him. Sovereignty belongs to Him and He is Potent over everything. There is no one worthy of worship except Allāh and we do not worship but Him alone. To Him belong all bounties, to Him belongs all Grace, and to Him is worthy praise accorded. There is no one worthy of worship except Allāh, to Whom we are sincere in devotion, even though the unbelievers disapprove of it."

4.

سُبْحَانَ اللهِ، الْحَمْدُ لِلهِ، اللهُ أَكْبَرُ

Subḥānallāh, al ḥamdulillāh, Allāhu akbar

"Glory be to Allāh, all praise be to Allāh, Allāh is the Greatest."

This should be said 33 times.

٣. لَا إِلَهَ إِلَّا اللَّهُ، وَحْدَهُ لَا شَرِيكَ لَهُ، لَهُ الْمُلْكُ وَلَهُ الْحَمْدُ، وَهُوَ عَلَى كُلِّ شَيْءٍ قَدِيرٌ، لَا إِلَهَ إِلَّا اللَّهُ، وَلَا نَعْبُدُ إِلَّا إِيَّاهُ، لَهُ النِّعْمَةُ، وَلَهُ الْفَضْلُ، وَلَهُ الثَّنَاءُ الْحَسَنُ، لَا إِلَهَ إِلَّا اللَّهُ مُخْلِصِينَ لَهُ الدِّينُ وَلَوْ كَرِهَ الْكَافِرُونَ.

٤. سُبْحَانَ اللَّهِ وَالْحَمْدُ لِلَّهِ، وَاللَّهُ أَكْبَرُ، ثَلَاثًا وَثَلَاثِينَ،

Then one should say:

لا إِلَهَ إلا اللهُ وَحْدَهُ لا شَرِيكَ لَه، لَهُ المُلْكُ ولَهُ الحَمْدُ وهُوَ عَلى كُلِّ شيءٍ قَدِير

Lā ilāha illallāhu waḥdahu lā sharīka lahu, lahul mulk, wa lahul ḥamd wa huwa ʿalā kulli shayʾin qadīr,

"None has the right to be worshipped except Allāh, Alone, without partner, to Him belongs all that exists, and to Him belongs the praise and He has power over all things."

which will complete the hundred.

117. The regular supererogatory prayers are ten *rakʿah* (units) which have been mentioned in the narration of Ibn ʿUmar ﵁, "I memorised from the Prophet ﷺ 10 units of prayer:

- Two before *Ẓuhr* and two after it.
- Two after *Maghrib* in his house.
- Two after *ʿIshāʾ* in his house.
- And two before *Fajr*. (Agreed upon).

وَيَقُولُ: لَا إِلَهَ إِلَّا اللَّهُ وَحْدَهُ لَا شَرِيكَ لَهُ، لَهُ الْمُلْكُ، وَلَهُ الْحَمْدُ، وَهُوَ عَلَى كُلِّ شَيْءٍ قَدِيرٌ. تَمَامَ الْمِائَةِ.

١١٧. وَالرَّوَاتِبُ الْمُؤَكَّدَةُ التَّابِعَةُ لِلْمَكْتُوبَاتِ عَشَرٌ:

وَهِيَ الْمَذْكُورَةُ فِي حَدِيثِ ابْنِ عُمَرَ رَضِيَ اللَّهُ عَنْهُمَا قَالَ: «حَفِظْتُ عَنْ رَسُولِ اللَّهِ ﷺ عَشْرَ رَكَعَاتٍ:

- رَكْعَتَيْنِ قَبْلَ الظُّهْرِ، وَرَكْعَتَيْنِ بَعْدَهَا.
- وَرَكْعَتَيْنِ بَعْدَ الْمَغْرِبِ فِي بَيْتِهِ.
- وَرَكْعَتَيْنِ بَعْدَ الْعِشَاءِ فِي بَيْتِهِ،
- وَرَكْعَتَيْنِ قَبْلَ الْفَجْرِ.» مُتَّفَقٌ عَلَيْهِ

بَابُ سُجُودِ السَّهْو والتِّلاوَة والشُّكْر

Chapter: Prostration of Forgetfulness, Recitation and Gratitude

118. The prostration of forgetfulness (*sahw*) is performed if:

1. A person added (*ziyādah*) a bowing, prostration, standing or sitting out of forgetfulness.

2. Or omitted (*naqṣ*) any of the things mentioned above. In this situation a person must make up what was omitted and prostrate for forgetfulness.

3. Or left out an obligation of the prayer out of forgetfulness.

4. Or doubted (*shakk*) in whether something was added or omitted.

It was reported that the Prophet ﷺ stood when he was meant to sit for the first *tashahhud* and prostrated (for it).

Likewise, he ﷺ "finished the *Ẓuhr* or *ʿAṣr* prayer after only completing two *rakʿah,* then the *Ṣaḥābah* reminded him ﷺ. He ﷺ then made up for the rest of the prayer and prostrated for forgetfulness."

بَابُ سُجُودِ السَّهْوِ وَالتِّلَاوَةِ وَالشُّكْرِ

١١٨. وَهُوَ مَشْرُوعٌ إِذَا:

١. زَادَ الإِنْسَانُ فِي صَلَاةٍ رُكُوعًا أَوْ سُجُودًا أَوْ قِيَامًا، أَوْ قُعُودًا، سَهْوًا.

٢. أَوْ نَقَصَ شَيْئًا مِنْ المذْكُورَاتِ: أَتَى بِهِ وَسَجَدَ لِلسَّهْوِ.

٣. أَوْ تَرَكَ وَاجِبًا مِنْ وَاجِبَاتِهَا سَهْوًا.

٤. أَوْ شَكَّ فِي زِيَادَةٍ أَوْ نُقْصَانٍ.

وَقَدْ ثَبَتَ أَنَّهُ صَلَّى اللهُ عَلَيْهِ وَسلَّم قَامَ عَنِ التَّشهُّدِ الأَوَّلِ فَسَجَدَ

وَسَلَّمَ مِنْ رَكْعَتَيْنِ مِنْ الظُّهْرِ أَوْ العَصْرِ، ثُمَّ ذَكَّرُوهُ، فَتَمَّمَ وَسَجَدَ لِلسَّهْوِ.

He ﷺ also once prayed 5 *rakʿah* for *Ẓuhr* after which it was said to him ﷺ, “Has the prayer increased (in the amount of *rakaʿah*)? So, he ﷺ replied, “And what are you referring to?”. They said, “You prayed 5 *rakʿah*” So, he ﷺ prostrated twice after he ﷺ did the *taslīm.*” (Agreed Upon)

The Prophet ﷺ said, “If one of you had doubts in your prayer and does not know how much he has prayed, whether 3 or 4, let him dispel this doubt and build upon certainty, then let him prostrate twice before he does the *taslīm.* If it was the case that he prayed 5, they (the two prostrations) will make his prayer even-numbered and if he prayed the exact amount (i.e. four) then they will be a humiliation for the devil.” (Muslim)

119. One can either prostrate before or after the *taslīm.*

120. The prostration of *tilāwah* (recitation) is recommended for the reciter and listener of the *Qurʾān* whether in prayer or not.

121. Likewise, if a person received a blessing or was averted from a trial then he should prostrate to Allāh سُبْحَانَهُ وَتَعَالَىٰ out of gratitude.

122. The ruling of the prostration of gratitude takes the same ruling as the prostration of recitation.

وصَلَّى الظُّهْرَ خَمْسًا فَقِيلَ لَهُ: أَزِيدَتِ الصَّلَاةُ؟ فَقَالَ: وَمَا ذَاكَ؟ قَالُوا: صَلَّيْتَ خَمْسًا، فَسَجَدَ سَجْدَتَيْنِ بَعْدَمَا سَلَّمَ. مُتَّفَقٌ عَلَيْهِ

وَقَالَ: «إِذَا شَكَّ أَحَدُكُمْ فِي صَلَاتِهِ، فَلَمْ يَدْرِ كَمْ صَلَّى: أَثَلَاثًا، أَمْ أَرْبَعًا؟ فَلْيَطْرَحِ الشَّكَّ، وَلْيَبْنِ عَلَى مَا اِسْتَيْقَنَ، ثُمَّ يَسْجُدُ سَجْدَتَيْنِ قَبْلَ أَنْ يُسَلِّمَ، فَإِنْ كَانَ صَلَّى خَمْسًا شَفَعْنَ صَلَاتَهُ. وَإِنْ كَانَ صَلَّى تَمَامًا كَانَتَا تَرْغِيمًا لِلشَّيْطَانِ.»

رَوَاهُ أَحْمَدُ وَمُسْلِمٌ

١١٩. وَلَهُ أَنْ يَسْجُدَ قَبْلَ السَّلَامِ أَوْ بَعْدَهُ.

١٢٠. وَيُسَنُّ سُجُودُ التِّلَاوَةِ لِلْقَارِئِ وَالْمُسْتَمِعِ فِي الصَّلَاةِ وَخَارِجِهَا.

١٢١. وَكَذَلِكَ إِذَا تَجَدَّدَتْ لَهُ نِعْمَةٌ، أَوْ اِنْدَفَعَتْ عَنْهُ نِقْمَةٌ، سَجَدَ لِلَّهِ شُكْرًا.

١٢٢. وَحُكْمُ سُجُودِ الشُّكْرِ كَسُجُودِ التِّلَاوَةِ.

بَابُ مُفْسِدَاتِ الصَّلاة ومَكْرُوهَاتِها

Chapter: The Nullifiers of Prayer and the Disliked Actions Therein

123. The prayer becomes nullified by the following:

1. Missing a pillar or condition whether accidentally, forgetfully or otherwise, unless he makes it up. Moreover, the prayer becomes nullified by intentionally leaving out an obligation.

2. Speaking intentionally.

3. Laughing.

4. To move excessively consecutively, without necessity. The standard for excessive movement is the custom (*ʿurf*).

These actions invalidate the prayer because in point 1, the act of worship is incomplete and in points 2-4 he committed a prohibited action.

بَابُ مُفْسِدَاتِ الصَّلَاةِ وَمَكْرُوهَاتِهَا

١٢٣. تَبْطُلُ الصَّلَاةُ

١. بِتَرْكِ رُكْنٍ أَوْ شَرْطٍ، وَهُوَ يَقْدِرُ عَلَيْهِ، عَمْدًا أَوْ سَهْوًا أَوْ جَهْلاً إِذَا لَمْ يَأْتِ بِهِ وَبِتَرْكِ وَاجِبٍ عَمْدًا.

٢. وَبِالْكَلَامِ عَمْدًا.

٣. وَبِالْقَهْقَهَةِ.

٤. وَبِالْحَرَكَةِ الكَثِيرَةِ عُرْفًا، المتَوالِيَةِ لِغَيْرِ ضَرُورَةٍ ;لِأَنَّهُ فِي الأَوَّلِ تَرَكَ مَا لَا تَتِمُّ العِبَادَةُ إِلَّا بِهِ، وَبِالْأَخِيرَاتِ فَعَلَ مَا يُنْهَى عَنْهُ فِيهَا.

124. It is disliked doing the following:

1. Turning around in prayer since the Prophet ﷺ was asked about turning around in prayer and said, "Turning around during prayer is something that the Devil snatches from one's prayer." (Bukhāri)

2. Playing frivolously (*ʿabath*).

3. Placing one's hands upon the hip/waist.

4. Interlocking one's fingers.

5. Clicking one's fingers.

6. Sit in the *iqʿāʾ* position like the *iqʿāʾ* of a dog.

7. Paying attention to something that distracts one from prayer.

8. Beginning the prayer whilst one's mind is focused on:

- holding back his urine or faeces
- the presence of food which one desires.

This is due to the saying of the Prophet ﷺ, "There is no prayer when food is present nor when one is holding back their urine or faeces." (Agreed upon)

١٢٤. وَيُكْرَهُ:

١. الِالْتِفَاتُ فِي الصَّلَاةِ؛ لِأَنَّ النَّبِيَّ ﷺ سُئِلَ عَنِ الِالْتِفَاتِ فِي الصَّلَاةِ فَقَالَ «هُوَ اِخْتِلَاسٌ يَخْتَلِسُهُ الشَّيْطَانُ مِنْ صَلَاةِ العَبْدِ.» رَوَاهُ البُخَارِيّ.

٢. وَيُكْرَهُ العَبَثُ.

٣. وَوَضْعُ اليَدِ عَلَى الخَاصِرَةِ.

٤. وَتَشْبِيكُ أَصَابِعِهِ.

٥. وَفَرْقَعَتُهَا.

٦. وَأَنْ يَجْلِسَ فِيهَا مُقْعِيًا كَإِقْعَاءِ الكَلْبِ

٧. وَأَنْ يَسْتَقْبِلَ مَا يُلْهِيهِ.

٨. أَوْ يَدْخُلَ فِيهَا وَقَلْبُهُ مُشْتَغِلٌ بِمُدَافَعَةِ الأَخْبَثَيْنِ، أَوْ بِحَضْرَةِ طَعَامٍ يَشْتَهِيهِ؛ لِقَوْلِهِ صلى الله عليه وسلم «لَا صَلَاةَ بِحَضْرَةِ طَعَامٍ، وَلَا هُوَ يُدَافِعُهُ الأَخْبَثَانِ.» متفق عليه

9. The Prophet ﷺ forbade that a person should lay down both of his forearms while prostrating. (Agreed upon)

٩. وَنَهَى النَّبِيُّ صَلَّى اللهُ عَليه وسلَّم أَنْ يَفْتَرِشَ الرَّجُلُ ذِرَاعَيْهِ فِي السُّجُود. متفق عليه

بَابُ صَلاةِ التَّطَوُّع

Chapter: Supererogatory Prayers

صَلاة الكُسُوف

Eclipse Prayer

125. The most recommended supererogatory prayer is the eclipse prayer because the Prophet ﷺ performed it and ordered it to be performed.

126. It is prayed in accordance to the description found in the ḥadīth of ʿĀʾishah رضي الله عنها, "that the Prophet ﷺ recited aloud for the eclipse prayer and did four bowings in two *rakaʿah* and four prostrations." (Agreed Upon)

صَلاة الوِتْر

The *Witr* Prayer

127. The *witr* prayer is a highly emphasised prayer (*sunnah muʾakkadah).* The Prophet ﷺ always performed it whether he was a resident or traveller. He also emphatically encouraged for others to perform it.

128. Its minimum is one *rakʿah.*

بَابُ صَلاةِ التَّطَوُّعِ

صَلاةُ الكُسُوفِ

١٢٥. وَآكَدُهَا: صَلَاةُ الكُسُوف; لِأَنَّ النَّبِيَّ ﷺ فَعَلَهَا وَأَمَرَ بِهَا.

١٢٦. وتُصَلَّى عَلَى صِفَةِ حَدِيثِ عَائِشَةَ: أن النَّبى ﷺ «جَهَرَ فِي صَلَاةِ الكُسُوفِ فِي قِرَاءَتِه فَصَلَّى أَرْبَعَ رَكَعَاتٍ فِي رَكْعَتَيْنِ، وَأَرْبَعَ سَجَدَاتٍ.» مُتَّفَقٌ عَلَيْه.

صَلاةُ الوِتْرِ

١٢٧. وَصَلَاةُ الوِتْرِ سُنَّةٌ مُؤَكَّدَةٌ. دَاوَمَ النَّبِيُّ ﷺ عَلَيْهِ حَضَرًا وَسَفَرًا. وَحَثَّ النَّاسَ عَلَيْهِ.

١٢٨. وَأَقَلُّهُ: رَكْعَةٌ.

129. Its maximum is eleven *rakʿah.*

130. Its time is from the *ʿIshāʾ* prayer until dawn.

131. It is more virtuous for it to be performed as one's last prayer of the night, since the Prophet ﷺ said, "Make your last prayer at night *witr* (odd)." (Agreed upon)

132. He ﷺ also said, "Whoever amongst you is afraid that he may not be able to get up at the end of the night should observe *Witr* (in the first part) and then sleep, and he who is confident of getting up and praying at night (i.e *Taḥajjud* prayer) should observe it at the end of it, for the recitation at the end of the night is witnessed and that is better." (Muslim)

صَلَاةُ الاسْتِسْقَاء

Prayer for Rain

133. The *istisqāʾ* prayer is recommended if people find themselves in difficult circumstances due to the loss of water.

134. It is prayed like the *ʿĪd* prayer in an open area.

١٢٩. وَأَكْثَرُهُ: إِحْدَى عَشْرَةَ.

١٣٠. وَوَقْتُهُ: مِنْ صَلَاةِ العِشَاءِ إِلَى طُلُوعِ الفَجْرِ.

١٣١. وَالْأَفْضَلُ: أَنْ يَكُونَ آخِرَ صَلَاتِهِ.

كَمَا قَالَ النَّبِيُّ ﷺ: «اِجْعَلُوا آخِرَ صَلَاتِكُمْ بِاللَّيْلِ وِتْرًا.» مُتَّفَقٌ عَلَيْهِ.

١٣٢. وقال: «مَنْ خَافَ أَلَّا يَقُومَ مِنْ آخِرِ اللَّيْلِ، فَلْيُوتِر أَوَّلَهُ، وَمَنْ طَمِعَ أَنْ يَقُومَ آخِرَهُ، فَلْيُوتِر آخِرَ اللَّيلِ، فَإِنَّ صَلاةَ آخِرِ اللَّيلِ مَشْهُودَةٌ، وَذَلِكَ أَفْضَلُ.» رَوَاهُ مُسْلِمٌ.

صَلَاةِ الاسْتِسْقَاءِ

١٣٣. وَصَلَاةُ الاسْتِسْقَاءِ: سُنَّةٌ إِذَا اُضْطُرَّ النَّاسُ لِفَقْدِ الماءِ.

١٣٤. وَتُفْعَلُ كَصَلَاةِ العِيدِ فِي الصَّحْرَاءِ.

135. A person should depart to the prayer humbled and abased.

136. The prayer consists of two *rakʿah.*

137. Then a single sermon should be delivered:

- Seeking forgiveness should be emphasised and verses that contain the command to seek forgiveness should be recited.
- Allāh should be implored and beseeched.
- One should not wait for a long time waiting for a sudden response.

138. Before leaving for the prayer, one should carry out the actions that repel evil and cause Allāh's ﷻ mercy to descend, such as:

- Seeking forgiveness.
- Repentance.
- Rectifying one's wrongdoing of others.
- Showing beneficence to others.
- And other means that Allāh ﷻ has made reasons for His mercy to descend and repellents for punishment. And Allāh ﷻ knows best.

١٣٥. وَيَخْرُجُ إِلَيْهَا: مُتَخَشِّعًا مُتَذَلِّلًا مُتَضَرِّعًا.

١٣٦. فَيُصَلِّي رَكْعَتَيْنِ.

١٣٧. ثُمَّ يَخْطُبُ خُطْبَةً وَاحِدَةً.

- يُكْثِرُ فِيهَا: الاسْتِغْفَارَ، وَقِرَاءَةَ الآيَاتِ التِي فِيهَا الأَمْرُ بِهِ.

- وَيُلِحُّ فِي الدُّعَاءِ.

- وَلَا يَسْتَبْطِئُ الإِجَابَةَ.

١٣٨. وَيَنْبَغِي قَبْلَ الخُرُوجِ إِلَيْهَا: فِعْلُ الأَسْبَابِ التِي تَدْفَعُ الشَّرَّ وَتُنْزِلُ الرَّحْمَةَ:

١. كَالِاسْتِغْفَارِ.

٢. وَالتَّوْبَةِ.

٣. وَالخُرُوجِ مِنْ المظَالِمِ.

٤. والإِحْسَانِ إِلَى الخَلْقِ.

٥. وَغَيْرِهَا مِنْ الأَسْبَابِ التي جَعَلَهَا اللهُ جَالِبَةً لِلرَّحْمَةِ، دَافِعَةً لِلنِّقْمَةِ. وَاللهُ أَعْلَم

أَوْقَاتُ النَّهْيِ

Prohibited Times to Pray

139. The prohibited times to pray the unrestricted recommended prayers (*al nawāfil al muṭlaqah*) are:

1. From *Fajr* until the sun rises above the horizon by the length of a spear.

2. From the *ʿAṣr* prayer until sunset.

3. From the time the sun has reached the zenith until it begins to descend. And Allāh ﷻ knows best.

أَوْقَاتُ النَّهْيِ

١٣٩. وَأَوْقَاتُ النَّهْيِ عَنْ النَّوَافِلِ المطْلَقَةِ:

١. مِنْ الفَجْرِ إِلَى أَنْ تَرْتَفِعَ الشَّمْسُ قَيْدَ رُمْحٍ.

٢. وَمِنْ صَلَاةِ العَصْرِ إِلَى الغُرُوبِ.

٣. وَمِنْ قِيَامِ الشَّمْسِ فِي كَبِدِ السَّمَاءِ إِلَى أَنْ تَزُولَ.

وَاللَّهُ أَعْلَمُ

بَابُ صَلاةِ الجَمَاعَةِ والإِمَامَة

Chapter: The Congregational Prayer and the Imamate

140. The congregational prayer is an individual obligation (*farḍ ʿayn*) for all five prayers. It is an obligation upon all men whether they are residents or travellers.

This is due to the statement of the Prophet ﷺ, "I have thought of giving the order for the prayer to be established, and then order a man to lead the people in prayer and then go with some men carrying a bundle of firewood to people who do not attend the prayer, then burn their homes with fire." (Agreed upon)

141. The minimum congregation consists of the Imām and the *Maʾmūm* (follower).

142. The larger the congregation is, the more beloved it is to Allāh ﷻ.

143. The Prophet ﷺ said, "A prayer offered in congregation is better than the prayer offered by a single person by 27 degrees." (Agreed Upon)

بَاب صَلَاةِ الجَمَاعَةِ وَالإِمَامَةِ

١٤٠. وَهِيَ فَرْضُ عَيْنٍ لِلصَّلَوَاتِ الخَمْسِ عَلَى الرِّجَالِ حَضَرًا وَسَفَرًا.

كَمَا قَالَ النَّبِي صَلَّى اللهُ عَلَيْهِ وَسَلَّمَ: «لَقَدْ هَمَمْتُ أَنْ آمُرَ بِالصَّلَاةِ فَتُقَامَ ثُمَّ آمُرَ رَجُلًا يَؤُمُّ النَّاسَ، ثُمَّ أَنْطَلِقَ بِرِجَالٍ مَعَهُمْ حُزَمٌ مِنْ حَطَبٍ إِلَى قَوْمٍ لَا يَشْهَدُونَ الصَّلَاةَ فَأُحَرِّقَ عَلَيْهِمْ بُيُوتَهُمْ بِالنَّارِ.» مُتَّفَقٌ عَلَيْهِ.

١٤١. وَأَقَلُّهَا: إِمَامٌ وَمَأْمُومٌ.

١٤٢. وَكُلَّمَا كَانَ أَكْثَرَ فَهُوَ أَحَبُّ إِلَى اللهِ.

وَقَالَ: «صَلَاةُ الجَمَاعَةِ أَفْضَلُ مِنْ صَلَاةِ الفَذِّ بِسَبْعٍ وَعِشْرِينَ دَرَجَةً.» مُتَّفَقٌ عَلَيْهِ

144. He also ﷺ said, “If you prayed in your homes and then came to a mosque that is praying in congregation, pray with them for verily that will be a voluntary prayer for you." (Abū Dāwūd, Tirmidhi and others)

145. Abū Hurayrah ﷺ reported in a *marfūʿ* narration, "The Imam is appointed so that he should be followed.

- If he says the *takbīr,* then say the *takbīr,* but do not say the *takbīr* until he has said the *takbīr.*
- And if he bows, then bow, but do not bow until he has bowed.
- And if he says, "*samiʿallāhu liman ḥamidah*" then say, "*Allāhumma rabbanā wa lakal ḥamd.*"
- And if he prostrates then prostrate, but do not prostrate until he has prostrated.
- And if he prays sitting, then all of you must pray sitting as well." (Abū Dāwūd. Its origin is found in the two *saḥīḥs*)

146. He ﷺ also said, "The following should lead the prayer:

- The most proficient in the recitation of the Qurʾān.
- If all of them are equal in recitation, then the most knowledgeable of the *sunnah* should lead.
- If all of them are equal in knowledge of the *sunnah,* then the one who made *hijrah* first should lead.

١٤٤. وَقَالَ صَلى الله علَيْهِ وسَلم: «إِذَا صَلَّيْتُمَا فِي رِحَالِكُمَا، ثُمَّ أَتَيْتُمَا مَسْجِدَ جَمَاعَةٍ فَصَلِّيَا مَعَهُمْ فَإِنَّهَا لَكُمْ نَافِلَةٌ.» رَوَاهُ أَهْلُ السُّنَنِ.

١٤٥. وعن أبي هريرة مرفوعًا: «إِنَّمَا جُعِلَ الإِمَامُ لِيُؤْتَمَّ بِهِ

- فَإِذَا كَبَّرَ فَكَبِّرُوا، وَلَا تُكَبِّرُوا حَتَّى يُكَبِّرَ.

- وَإِذَا رَكَعَ فَارْكَعُوا، وَلَا تَرْكَعُوا حَتَّى يَرْكَعَ.

- وَإِذَا قَالَ: سَمِعَ اللَّهُ لِمَنْ حَمِدَهُ، فَقُولُوا: اللَّهُمَّ رَبَّنَا وَلَكَ الحَمْدُ.

- وَإِذَا سَجَدَ فَاسْجُدُوا، وَلَا تَسْجُدُوا حَتَّى يَسْجُدَ.

- وَإِذَا صَلَّى قَاعِدًا فَصَلُّوا قُعُودًا أَجْمَعُونَ.» رَوَاهُ أَبُو دَاوُدَ وَأَصْلُهُ فِي الصَّحِيحَيْنِ.

١٤٦. وقال: «يَؤُمُّ القَومَ أَقْرَؤُهُمْ لِكِتَابِ اللهِ، فَإِنْ كَانُوا فِي القِرَاءَةِ سَوَاءٌ فَأَعْلَمُهُمْ بِالسُّنَّةِ،

- If all of them made *hijrah* at the same time, then the more senior in Islam (i.e. in terms of when he became Muslim) or the more senior in age should lead.
- No man must lead another in prayer where (the latter) has authority or sit in his place of honour in his house, without his permission." (Muslim)

147. And it is required that:

1. The Imām prays in front of the congregation.
2. The followers pray in a straight line, leaving no gaps.
3. The followers complete the rows, starting with the first.

148. Whoever prays a *rakʿah* by himself behind a row (whilst in congregation) without a valid reason must repeat their prayer.

149. Ibn ʿAbbās ﷺ said, "One night I prayed with the Prophet ﷺ and I prayed on his left-hand side. Then the Prophet ﷺ grabbed my head from behind and made me stand on his right-hand side." (Agreed upon)

150. The Prophet said ﷺ, "If you heard the *Iqāmah* then walk to the prayer calmly and with dignity and do not rush. Whatever you have caught of the prayer then pray it, and whatever you have missed of the prayer then complete it (*fa atimmū*)." (Agreed upon)

فَإِنْ كَانُوا فِي الْهِجْرَةِ سَوَاءٌ فَأَقْدَمُهُمْ سِلْمًا أو سنًّا. وَلَا يَؤُمَّنَّ الرَّجُلُ الرَّجُلَ فِي سُلْطَانِهِ، وَلَا يَقْعُدْ فِي بَيْتِهِ عَلَى تكْرِمَتِهِ إِلَّا بِإِذْنِهِ.» رَوَاهُ مُسْلِمٌ

١٤٧. وَيَنْبَغِي:

١. أَنْ يَتَقَدَّمَ الإِمَامُ

٢. وَأَنْ يَتَرَاصَّ المأْمُومُونَ

٣. وَيُكْمِلُونَ الأَوَّلَ بِالْأَوَّلِ.

١٤٨. وَمَنْ صَلَّى فَذًّا رَكْعَةً خَلْفَ الصَّفِّ لِغَيْرِ عُذْرٍ أَعَادَ صَلَاتَهُ.

١٤٩. وَقَالَ اِبْنُ عَبَّاسٍ: «صَلَّيْتُ مَعَ النَّبِيِّ ﷺ ذَاتَ لَيْلَةٍ، فَقُمْتُ عَنْ يَسَارِهِ فَأَخَذَ بِرَأْسِي مِنْ وَرَائِي فَجَعَلَنِي عَنْ يَمِينِهِ.» مُتَّفَقٌ عَلَيْهِ.

١٥٠. وَقَال «إِذَا سَمِعْتُمْ الإِقَامَةَ فَامْشُوا إِلَى الصَّلَاةِ وَعَلَيْكُمْ السَّكِينَةُ وَالْوَقَارُ، وَلَا تُسْرِعُوا، فَمَا أَدْرَكْتُمْ فَصَلُّوا، وَمَا فَاتَكُمْ فَأَتِمُّوا.» مُتَّفَقٌ عَلَيْهِ

151. The Prophet ﷺ also said, "If you enter the prayer and the Imām is in a particular position, then do exactly what the Imām is doing." (Tirmidhi)

١٥١. وفي الترمذي: «إِذَا أَتَى أَحَدُكُمْ الصَّلَاةَ وَالإِمَامُ عَلَى حَالٍ، فَلْيَصْنَعْ كَمَا يَصْنَعُ الإِمَامُ.»

بَابُ صَلاةِ أَهْلِ الأَعْذَار

Chapter: The Prayer of Those with Excuses

152. The ill are excused from attending the congregational prayer.

153. If standing in prayer increases one's illness, then one should pray sitting. And if one cannot manage sitting, then one should pray on their side due to the statement of the Prophet ﷺ, "Pray standing, but if you cannot then pray sitting and if you cannot do that, then pray on your side." (Bukhāri)

154. If it becomes difficult upon him (i.e. the sick) to pray every prayer in its designated time one can combine *Ẓuhr* with *ʿAṣr* and *Maghrib* with *ʿIshāʾ* in either of the two prayer times.

صَلاةُ الْمُسَافِر

The Prayer of the Traveller

155. It is also permissible for the traveller to combine their prayers.

156. It is recommended to shorten the four-unit prayers to two units.

157. One can also break their fast in Ramaḍān.

بَابُ صَلَاةِ أَهْلِ الأَعْذَار

صَلَاةُ المَرِيضِ

١٥٢. وَالْمَرِيضُ يُعْفَى عَنْهُ حُضُورُ الجَمَاعَةِ.

١٥٣. وَإِذَا كَانَ القِيَامُ يُزِيدُ مَرَضَهُ: صَلَّى جَالِسًا، فَإِنْ لَمْ يُطِقْ: فَعَلَى جَنْبٍ؛ لِقَوْلِ النَّبِيِّ ﷺ لِعِمْرَانَ بْنِ حُصَيْنٍ: «صَلِّ قَائِمًا، فَإِنْ لَمْ تَسْتَطِعْ فَقَاعِدًا، فَإِنْ لَمْ تَسْتَطِعْ فَعَلَى جَنْبٍ.» رَوَاهُ البُخَارِيُّ.

١٥٤. وإن شقَّ عَلَيْهِ فِعْلُ كُلِّ مِنْ صَلَاةٍ فِي وَقْتِهَا، فَلَهُ الجَمْعُ بَيْنَ الظُّهْرِ والعَصْرِ، وَبَيْنَ العِشَاءَيْنِ، فِي وَقْتِ إِحْدَاهُما.

صَلَاةُ المُسَافِرِ

١٥٥. وَكَذَا المسَافِرُ يَجُوزُ لَهُ الجَمْعُ.

١٥٦. وَيُسَنُّ لَهُ القَصْرُ لِلصَّلَاةِ الرُّبَاعِيَّةِ إِلَى رَكْعَتَيْنِ.

١٥٧. وَلَهُ الفِطْرُ بِرَمَضَان.

صَلاةُ الخَوْف

The Prayer of the One in the State of Fear

158. It is permissible to pray the prayer of fear in accordance with all the ways the Prophet ﷺ is reported to have prayed it.

159. Amongst the ways that one can perform this prayer can be found in the narration of Ṣāliḥ bin Khawwāt ؓ regarding the one who prayed the prayer of fear with the Prophet ﷺ on the day of *Dhāt Riqāʿ*,

- "A group of people made a row behind the Prophet ﷺ whilst another group were facing the enemy.
- The Prophet ﷺ then prayed a *rakʿah* with those behind him.
- Then the Prophet ﷺ stood up whilst the group behind him completed their prayers on their own (whilst the Prophet ﷺ remained standing).
- Then the group left to face the enemy.
- Then the other group came and prayed the last *rakaʿah* of the Prophet ﷺ with him, and then he sat waiting whilst the row behind him completed their prayer. Then he made the *taslīm* with them." (Agreed upon)

صَلَاةُ الخَوْفِ

١٥٨. وَتَجُوزُ صَلَاةُ الخَوْفِ عَلَى كُلِّ صِفَةٍ صَلَّاهَا النَّبِيُّ ﷺ

١٥٩. فَمِنْهَا: حَدِيثُ صَالِحِ بْنِ خَوَّاتٍ عَمَّنْ صَلَّى مَعَ النَّبِيِّ ﷺ يَوْمَ ذَاتِ الرِّقَاعِ صَلَاةَ الخَوْفِ

- أَنَّ طَائِفَةً صَلَّتْ مَعَهُ، وَطَائِفَةً وِجَاهَ العَدُوِّ.
- فَصَلَّى بِالذِينَ مَعَهُ رَكْعَةً.
- ثُمَّ ثَبَتَ قَائِمًا وَأَتَمُّوا لِأَنْفُسِهِمْ.
- ثُمَّ اِنْصَرَفُوا وَصَفُّوا وِجَاهَ العَدُوِّ.
- وَجَاءَتْ الطَّائِفَةُ الأُخْرَى فَصَلَّى بِهِمْ الرَّكْعَةَ التِي بَقِيَتْ، ثُمَّ ثَبَتَ جَالِسًا وَأَتَمُّوا لِأَنْفُسِهِمْ. مُتَّفَقٌ عَلَيه

160. If their fear becomes intensified then they should pray whilst on foot or while riding, facing the *qiblah* or other than it, making motions for bowing and prostration.

161. This also applies to a person who fears for themselves; they should pray according to their circumstances. One should do that which the situation demands such as fleeing and the like.

The Prophet ﷺ said, "If I command you to do something then do it according to the best of your abilities." (Agreed upon)

١٦٠. وَإِذَا اِشْتَدَّ الخَوْفُ: صَلُّوا رِجَالًا وَرُكْبَانًا إِلَى القِبْلَةِ وَإِلَى غَيْرِهَا، يُومِئُونَ بِالرُّكُوعِ وَالسُّجُودِ.

١٦١. وَكَذَلِكَ كُلُّ خَائِفٍ عَلَى نَفْسِهِ يُصَلِّي عَلَى حَسَبِ حَالِهِ، وَيَفْعَلُ كُلَّ مَا يَحْتَاجُ إِلَى فِعْلِهِ مِنْ هَرَبٍ أَوْ غَيْرِهِ.

قَالَ ﷺ: «إِذَا أَمَرْتُكُمْ بِأَمْرٍ فَائْتُوا مِنْهُ مَا اِسْتَطَعْتُمْ.» مُتَّفَقٌ عَلَيْه

بَابُ صَلَاةِ الجُمُعَة

Chapter: *Jumuʿah* Prayer

162. Everyone who is required to attend the congregational prayer must also attend the Friday prayer if he is *mustawṭin* (i.e. lives in a residential area) surrounded by buildings.

163. From its conditions:

1. It must be performed in its allocated time.
2. It must to be done in a populated area.
3. It must be preceded by two *khuṭbahs.*

164. Jābir ﷺ reported that when the Prophet ﷺ performed the Friday sermon:

- His eyes would become red, his voice would rise, and his anger would increase as if he was warning of an invading army saying, "The enemy has made a morning attack on you. The enemy has made an evening attack on you."

بَابُ صَلَاةِ الجُمُعَةِ

١٦٢. كُلُّ مَنْ لَزِمَتْهُ الجَمَاعَةُ لَزِمَتْهُ الجُمْعَةُ إِذَا كَانَ مُسْتَوْطِنًا بِبِنَاءٍ.

١٦٣. وَمِنْ شَرْطِهَا

١. فِعْلُهَا فِي وَقْتِهَا.

٢. وَأَنْ تَكُونَ بِقَرْيَةٍ.

٣. وَأَنْ يَتَقَدَّمَهَا خُطْبَتَانِ.

١٦٤. وَعَنْ جَابِرٍ قَالَ: «كَانَ النَّبِيُّ ﷺ إِذَا خَطَبَ:

- اِحْمَرَّتْ عَيْنَاهُ، وَعَلَا صَوْتُهُ، وَاشْتَدَّ غَضَبُهُ، حَتَّى كَأَنَّهُ مُنْذِرُ جَيْشٍ يَقُولُ: صَبَّحَكُمْ وَمَسَّاكُمْ.

- He used to say,
- "*Amma baʿd, fa inna khayral ḥadīthi kitābullāh, wa khayral hadyī hadyu Muḥammadin, wa sharral umūri muḥdathatuha, wa kulla bidʿatin ḍalālah.*" (To proceed, verily the best speech is the book of Allāh, and the best guidance is the guidance of Muḥammad, and the worst matters are the newly invented matters, and every innovation is a misguidance.") Reported by Muslim.
- In another narration it states, "In the sermon of the Prophet ﷺ he used to praise Allāh ﷻ and glorify Him and then used to say after that the aforementioned whilst his voice was raised."
- In another narration he used to say, "*Man-yahdillāhu fa lā muḍilla lah, wa man-yuḍlil fa lā hādiya lah.*" (Whomever Allāh guides no one can lead astray and whomever Allāh misguides no one can guide.)
- He also said, "Verily, the length of the prayer of a person and the shortness of his sermon are a sign of his *fiqh* (understanding)." (Muslim)

165. It is recommended that he gives his sermon on a pulpit (*minbar*).

166. When he climbs the *minbar* he should face the people and then greet them.

- وَيَقُولُ: «أَمَّا بَعْدُ، فَإِنَّ خَيْرَ الحَدِيثِ كِتَابُ اللَّهِ، وَخَيْرَ الهَدْيِ هَدْيُ مُحَمَّدٍ، وَشَرَّ الأُمُورِ مُحْدَثَاتُهَا، وَكُلَّ بِدْعَةٍ ضَلَالَةٌ.» رَوَاهُ مُسْلِمٌ.

- وَفِي لَفْظٍ لَهُ، كَانَتْ خُطْبَةُ النَّبِيِّ ﷺ يَوْمَ الجُمُعَةِ يَحْمَدُ اللهَ وَيُثْنِي عَلَيْهِ، ثُمَّ يَقُولُ عَلَى إِثْرِ ذَلِكَ، وَقَدْ عَلا صَوْتُهُ.

- وَفِي رِوَايَةٍ لَهُ، «مَنْ يَهْدِ اللَّهُ فَلَا مُضِلَّ لَهُ، وَمَنْ يُضْلِلْ فَلَا هَادِيَ لَهُ.»

- وَقَالَ: «إِنَّ طُولَ صَلَاةِ الرَّجُلِ، وَقِصَرَ خُطْبَتِهِ مَئِنَّةٌ مِنْ فِقْهِهِ.» رَوَاهُ مُسْلِمٌ.

١٦٥. وَيُسْتَحَبُّ أَنْ يَخْطُبَ عَلَى مِنْبَرٍ.

١٦٦. فَإِذَا صَعِدَ أَقْبَلَ عَلَى النَّاسِ فَسَلَّمَ عَلَيْهِمْ.

167. Then he should sit and let the caller to prayer call the *adhān.*

168. Then he should stand and give the sermon.

169. Then he should sit.

170. Then he should give the second sermon.

171. Then the prayer should be established.

172. The prayer consists of two units.

173. The Imām should recite aloud.

174. In the first unit, it is recommended to recite *Sūrah al Aʿlā* and in the second, *Sūrah al Ghāshiyah* or *Sūrah al Jumuʿah* in the first and *Sūrah al Munāfiqūn* in the second.

175. It is recommended for the one who attends the prayer to:

1. Bathe
2. Perfume himself
3. Wear his best clothes
4. Go to the mosque early

١٦٧. ثُمَّ يَجْلِسُ وَيُؤَذِّنُ المؤَذِّنُ.

١٦٨. ثُمَّ يَقُومُ فَيَخْطُبُ.

١٦٩. ثُمَّ يَجْلِسُ.

١٧٠. ثُمَّ يَخْطُبُ الخُطْبَةَ الثَّانِيَةَ.

١٧١. ثُمَّ تُقَامُ الصَّلَاةُ.

١٧٢. فَيُصَلِّي بِهِمْ رَكْعَتَيْنِ.

١٧٣. يَجْهَرُ فِيهِمَا بِالْقِرَاءَةِ.

١٧٤. يَقْرَأُ فِي الأُولَى بِـ: «سَبِّحْ»، وَفِي الثَّانِيَةِ بِـ: «الغَاشِيَةِ»، أَوْ بِـ: «الجُمْعَةِ وَالْمُنَافِقِينَ.»

١٧٥. وَيُسْتَحَبُّ لِمَنْ أَتَى الجُمْعَةَ أَنْ:

١. يَغْتَسِلَ.

٢. وَيَتَطَيَّبَ.

٣. وَيَلْبَسَ أَحْسَنَ ثِيَابِهِ.

٤. وَيُبَكِّرَ إِلَيْهَا.

176. The Prophet ﷺ said, "When the Imām is delivering the sermon on Friday and you say to your companion to keep quiet, then indeed you have spoken foolishly (i.e. committed a sin)." (Agreed Upon)

177. It is also reported that a man entered the mosque when the Prophet ﷺ was delivering the sermon, so he ﷺ asked the man, "Have you prayed?" The man said, "No." The Prophet ﷺ then said, "Stand and pray two units of prayer." (Agreed upon)

١٧٦. وَفِي الصَّحِيحَيْنِ: «إِذَا قُلْتَ لِصَاحِبِكَ: أَنْصِتْ يَوْمَ الجُمْعَةِ، وَالْإِمَامُ يَخْطُبُ، فَقَدْ لَغَوْتَ.»

١٧٧. وَدَخَلَ رَجُلٌ يَوْمَ الجُمْعَةِ وَالنَّبِيُّ صَلّى اللهُ عَلَيْهِ وسَلَّم يَخْطُبُ، فَقَالَ: صَلَّيْتَ؟ قَالَ: لَا، قَالَ: «قُمْ فَصَلِّ رَكْعَتَيْنِ.» مُتَّفَقٌ عَلَيْه

بَابُ صَلاةِ العِدَيْن

Chapter: The ʿĪd Prayers

178. The Prophet ﷺ commanded everyone to attend the prayer, even young girls (*awātiq*) and menstruating women so that they can witness the blessings and supplications of the Muslims. However, menstruating women should avoid the *muṣallā* (place of prayer). (Agreed upon)

179. The time of the prayer begins from when the sun is above the horizon by the length of a spear up until the zenith.

180. The recommended actions are:

1. For the prayer to be performed in an open area.
2. To hasten the *Aḍḥā* prayer.
3. To delay the *Fiṭr* prayer.
4. To have an odd amount of dates before the *Fiṭr* prayer.
5. To wash and perfume oneself for the prayer.
6. To wear one's best clothes.
7. To go to the place of prayer one way and to return home using another path.

بَابُ صَلَاةِ العِيدَيْنِ

١٧٨. أَمَرَ النَّبِيُّ ﷺ النَّاسَ بِالْخُرُوجِ إِلَيْهِمَا حَتَّى العَوَاتِقَ، وَالْحُيَّضَ يَشْهَدْنَ الخَيْرَ وَدَعْوَةَ المُسْلِمِينَ، وَيَعْتَزِلُ الحُيَّضُ المُصَلَّى. مُتَّفَقٌ عَلَيْهِ.

١٧٩. وَوَقْتُهَا: مِنِ ارْتِفَاعِ الشَّمْسِ قَيْدَ رُمْحٍ إِلَى الزَّوَالِ.

١٨٠. وَالسُّنَّةُ:

١. فِعْلُهَا فِي الصَّحْرَاءِ.

٢.وَتَعْجِيلُ الأَضْحَى.

٣. وَتَأْخِيرُ الفِطْرِ.

٤. وَالْفِطْرُ فِي الفِطْرِ خَاصَّةً قَبْلَ الصَّلَاةِ بِتَمَرَاتٍ وِتْرًا.

٥. وَأَنْ يَتَنَظَّفَ وَيَتَطَيَّبَ لَهَا.

٦. وَيَلْبَسَ أَحْسَنَ ثِيَابِهِ.

٧. وَيَذْهَبَ مِنْ طَرِيقٍ، وَيَرْجِعَ مِنْ آخَرَ.

181. The prayer consists of two units.

182. It has no *adhān* and no *iqāmah.*

183. There are seven *takbīrs* in the first *rakʿah*, including the initial *takbīr.*

184. And in the second *rakʿah,* there are five *takbīrs* not including the *takbīr* said from rising from prostration.

185. One should raise their hands with each *takbīr.*

186. One should praise Allāh ﷻ and send salutations upon the Prophet ﷺ between each *takbīr.*

187. Then recite *al Fātiḥah* followed by another chapter.

188. The prayer is recited aloud.

189. As soon as the Imām finishes, he should give two sermons like the two sermons for *Jumuʿah.*

190. However, in this *khuṭbah* the Imām should mention rulings (*aḥkām*) that are suitable for the occasion.

١٨١. فَيُصَلِّي بِهِمْ رَكْعَتَيْنِ.

١٨٢. بِلَا أَذَانٍ وَلَا إِقَامَةٍ.

١٨٣. يُكَبِّرُ فِي الأُولَى: سَبْعًا بِتَكْبِيرَةِ الإِحْرَامِ.

١٨٤. وَفِي الثَّانِيَةِ: خَمْسًا سِوَى تَكْبِيرَةِ القِيَامِ.

١٨٥. يَرْفَعُ يَدَيْهِ مَعَ كُلِّ تَكْبِيرَةٍ،

١٨٦. ويَحمَدُ اللهَ وَيُصَلِّيَ عَلَى النَّبِيِّ صلى الله عليه وسلم بَيْنَ كُلِّ تَكْبِيرَتَيْنِ،

١٨٧. ثُمَّ يَقْرَأُ الفَاتِحَةَ وَسُورَةً،

١٨٨. يَجْهَرُ بِالقِرَاءَةِ فِيهَا،

١٨٩. فَإِذَا سَلَّمَ خَطَبَ بِهِمْ خُطْبَتَيْنِ، كَخُطْبَتَيِ الجُمْعَةِ.

١٩٠. إِلَّا أَنَّهُ يَذْكُرُ فِي كُلِّ خُطْبَةٍ الأَحْكَامَ المنَاسِبَةَ لِلْوَقْتِ.

191. It is recommended to:

1. Make the unrestricted *takbīr* (*takbīr muṭlaq*):
- During the night before both ᶜĪds.
- Likewise, during the first ten days of *Dhul Ḥijjah.*

2. The restricted *takbīr* (*takbir muqayyad*) should be said after each obligatory prayer from the *Fajr* of the day of *ᶜArafah* until the *ᶜAṣr* prayer of the last day of *Tashrīq.*

The format for the *takbīr* is:

اللهُ أَكْبَرُ اللهُ أَكْبَرُ لا إِلَهَ إِلا اللهُ واللهُ أَكْبَرُ اللهُ أَكْبَرُ وللهِ الْحَمْد

Allāhu Akbar, Allāhu Akbar lā ilāha illallāh wallāhu Akbar, Allāhu Akbar, wa lillāhil ḥamd.

١٩١. وَيُسْتَحَبُّ:

١. التَّكْبِيرُ المطْلَقُ:

- لَيْلَتَيْ العِيدِ،

- وَفِي كُلِّ عَشْرِ ذِي الحِجَّةِ.

٢. وَالْمُقَيَّدُ: عَقِبَ الْمَكْتُوبَاتِ مِنْ صَلَاةِ فَجْرِ يَوْمِ عَرَفَةَ إِلَى عَصْرِ آخِرِ أَيَّامِ التَّشْرِيقِ.

وَصِفَتُهُ «اللَّهُ أَكْبَرُ، اللَّهُ أَكْبَرُ لَا إِلَهَ إِلَّا اللَّهُ، وَاللَّهُ أَكْبَرُ، اللَّهُ أَكْبَرُ، وَلِلَّهِ الحَمْدُ».

كِتَابُ الجَنَائِز

The Book of Funerals

192. The Prophet ﷺ said, "Instruct those who are about to pass away to say *lā ilāha illa-llāh.*" (Muslim)

193. The Prophet ﷺ said, "Recite Sūrah *Yā Sīn* upon the dead (i.e. those about to die)." (Nasāʾi and Abū Dāwūd)

194. The preparation for the deceased by washing him, shrouding him, praying for him, carrying and burying him are all a communal obligation (*farḍ kifāyah*).

195. The Prophet ﷺ said, "Hasten with the Janāzah, for if it was righteous then you are taking it toward something good, and if it was otherwise, then it is an evil of which you are relieving yourselves from." (Agreed upon)

196. The Prophet ﷺ also said, "The believer's soul is suspended by his debt until it is settled for him." (Aḥmad and Tirmidhi)

197. The obligation of the *kafan* (shroud) is that it should cover the whole body, apart from the head of the *Muḥrim* (one who is in a state of *iḥrām*) and the face of the *Muḥrimah* (female in the state of *iḥrām*).

كِتَابُ الجَنَائِزِ

١٩٢. قَالَ النَّبِيُّ ﷺ: «لَقِّنُوا مَوْتَاكُمْ لَا إِلَهَ إِلَّا اللَّهُ.» رَوَاهُ مُسْلِمٌ.

١٩٣. وَقَالَ: «اِقْرَءُوا عَلَى مَوْتَاكُمْ يس.» رَوَاهُ النَّسَائِيُّ وَأَبُو دَاوُدَ.

١٩٤. وتجهيز الميت، بِغَسْلِهِ وَتَكْفِينِهِ وَالصَّلَاةِ عَلَيْهِ وَحَمْلِهِ وَدَفْنِهِ، فَرْضُ كِفَايَةٍ.

١٩٥. قَالَ النَّبِيُّ ﷺ: «أَسْرِعُوا بِالْجِنَازَةِ، فَإِنْ تَكُ صَالِحَةً فَخَيْرٌ تُقَدِّمُونَهَا إِلَيْهِ، وَإِنْ كَانَتْ غَيْرَ ذَلِكَ فَشَرٌّ تَضَعُونَهُ عَنْ رِقَابِكُمْ.»

١٩٦. وَقَالَ: «نَفْسُ المؤْمِنِ مُعَلَّقَةٌ بِدَيْنِهِ حَتَّى يُقْضَى عَنْهُ.» رَوَاهُ أَحْمَدُ وَالتِّرْمِذِيُّ.

١٩٧. وَالْوَاجِبُ فِي الكَفَنِ: ثَوْبٌ يَسْتُرُ جَمِيعَهُ، سِوَى رَأْسِ المحْرِمِ، وَوَجْهِ المحْرِمَةِ

198. The description of the prayer is as follows:

1. One should say the *takbīr* and then recite the *Fātiḥah.*
2. Then make *takbīr* again and send salutations upon the Prophet ﷺ.
3. Then make *takbīr* again and pray for the deceased by saying:

اللهُمَّ اغْفِرْ لِحَيِّنَا وَمَيِّتِنَا وَصَغِيرِنَا وَكَبِيرِنَا وَشَاهِدِنَا وَغَائِبِنَا وَذَكَرِنَا وَأُنْثَانَا اللهُمَّ مَنْ أَحْيَيْتَهُ مِنَّا فَأَحْيِهِ عَلَى الإِسْلام وَمَنْ تَوَفَّيْتَهُ مِنَّا فَتَوَفَّهُ عَلَى الإِيْمَان

Allāhumma-ghfir li ḥayyinā wa mayyitinā wa ṣaghīrinā wa kabīrinā wa shāhidinā wa ghāʾibinā wa dhakarina wa unthāna. Allāhumma man aḥyaytahu minnā fa-aḥyihi ʿalal Islām, wa man tawaffaytahu minnā fa tawaffahu ʿalal īmān.

O Allāh, forgive our living and our dead, our young and our old, our present and our absent, our males and our females. O Allāh, for the one You continue to give life amongst us, keep him alive upon Islām. And for the one that You grant death to amongst us, let him die upon faith.

١٩٨. وَصِفَةُ الصَّلَاةِ عَلَيْهِ:

١. أَنْ يَقُومَ فَيُكَبِّرَ فَيَقْرَأَ الفَاتِحَةَ.

٢. ثُمَّ يُكَبِّرَ وَيُصَلِّيَ عَلَى النَّبِيِّ ﷺ .

٣. ثُمَّ يُكَبِّرَ وَيَدْعُوَ لِلْمَيِّتِ فَيَقُولَ:

«اللَّهُمَّ اِغْفِرْ لِحَيِّنَا وَمَيِّتِنَا، وَصَغِيرِنَا وَكَبِيرِنَا وَشَاهِدِنَا وَغَائِبِنَا، وَذَكَرِنَا وَأُنْثَانَا، اللَّهُمَّ مَنْ أَحْيَيْتَهُ مِنَّا فَأَحْيِهِ عَلَى الإِسْلَامِ، وَمَنْ تَوَفَّيْتَهُ فَتَوَفَّهُ عَلَى الإِيمَانِ.»

اللهُمَّ اغْفِرْ لَهُ وَارْحَمْهُ وَعَافِهِ وَاعْفُ عَنْهُ وَأَكْرِمْ نُزُلَهُ وَوَسِّعْ مُدْخَلَهُ وَاغْسِلْهُ بِالْمَاءِ وَالثَّلْجِ والبَرَدِ وَنَقِّهِ مِنَ الْخَطَايَا كَمَا نَقَّيْتَ الثَّوْبَ الأَبْيَضَ مِنَ الدَنَسِ اللهُمَّ لا تَحْرِمْنَا أَجْرَهُ ولا تَفْتِنَّا بَعْدَهُ واغْفِرْ لَنَا وَلَهُ

Allāhumma-ghfir lahu war-ḥamhu, wa ʿāfihi waʿfu ʿanhu, wa akrim nuzulahu, wa wassiʿ mudkhalu wa-ghsilhu bil-māʾi wath-thalji wal barad, wa naqqihi minal khaṭāya kamā naqqayta-thawbal abyaḍa minad-danas. Allāhumma lā taḥrimnā ajrahu wa lā taftinnā baʿdah, wagh-fir lanā wa lahu.

O Allāh, forgive him, have mercy on him, pardon him and make him safe, and make his resting place an honourable one and make his entryway expansive. Clean him with water, snow and hail and purify him from sins like a white garment is cleansed from dirt. O Allāh, do not deny us its reward and do not put us to test after it.

If the deceased was a minor, one should say after the general supplication:

اللهُمَّ اجْعَلْهُ ذُخراً لِوَالِدَيْهِ وَفَرَطاً وشَفِيعاً مُجَاباً اللهُمَّ ثَقِّلْ بِهِ مَوَازِينَهُمَا وَأَعْظِمْ بِهِ أُجُورَهُمَا وَاجْعَلْهُ فِي كَفَالَةِ إِبْرَاهِيمَ وَقِهِ بِرَحْمَتِكَ عَذَابَ الجَحِيم

«اللَّهُمَّ اِغْفِرْ لَهُ، وَارْحَمْهُ، وَعَافِهِ، وَاعْفُ عَنْهُ، وَأَكْرِمْ نُزُلَهُ، وَوَسِّعْ مُدْخَلَهُ، وَاغْسِلْهُ بِالْمَاءِ وَالثَّلْجِ وَالْبَرَدِ، وَنَقِّهِ مِنْ الذُّنُوبِ كَمَا يُنَقَّى الثَّوْبُ الأَبْيَضُ مِنْ الدَّنَسِ، اللَّهُمَّ لَا تَحْرِمْنَا أَجْرَهُ، وَلَا تَفْتِنَّا بَعْدَهُ، وَاغْفِرْ لَنَا وَلَهُ.»

وَإِنْ كَانَ صَغِيرًا قَالَ بَعْدَ الدُّعَاءِ العَامّ: «اللَّهُمَّ اِجْعَلْهُ فَرَطًا لِوَالِدَيْهِ، وَذُخْرًا، وَشَفِيعًا مُجَابًا، اللَّهُمَّ ثَقِّلْ بِهِ مَوَازِينَهُمَا، وَأَعْظِمْ بِهِ أُجُورَهُمَا، وَاجْعَلْهُ فِي كَفَالَةِ إِبْرَاهِيمَ، وَقِهِ بِرَحْمَتِكَ عَذَابَ الجَحِيمِ.»

Allāhumma-jʿalhu dhukhran li wālidayhi wa faraṭan wa shafīʿan mujāban. Allāhumma thaqqil bihi mawāzīnahuma wa aʿaẓim bihi ujūrahuma wajʿalhu fī kafālati Ibrāhīm wa qihi biraḥmatika ʿadhābal-jaḥīm.

O Allāh, make him a stored treasure for his parents and a predecessor and an accepted intercessor. O Allāh, make their scales heavy because of him and make their rewards greater. And place him under the care of Ibrahim, and save him by Your mercy, from the punishment of the fire.

199. Then one should do another *takbīr* and say the *taslīm.*

200. The Prophet ﷺ said, "If any Muslim dies and forty men who associate nothing with Allāh ﷻ offer prayer on him, Allāh ﷻ will accept them as intercessors for him." (Muslim)

201. He ﷺ also said, "He who attends a funeral until the prayer is offered for the dead, will have the reward of one *qīrāṭ*, and he who attends (and stays) until he is buried will have the reward of two *qīrāṭ*. It was asked, "What are the two *qīrāṭ*?" He ﷺ said, "Like two huge mountains." (Agreed upon)

202. The Prophet ﷺ prohibited:

1. to plaster/whitewash the grave.
2. to sit upon it.
3. to build a structure upon it. (Muslim)

١٩٩. ثُمَّ يُكَبِّرَ وَيُسَلِّمَ.

٢٠٠. وَقَالَ النَّبِيُّ ﷺ: «مَا مِنْ رَجُلٍ مُسْلِمٍ يَمُوتُ، فَيَقُومُ عَلَى جِنَازَتِهِ أَرْبَعُونَ رَجُلًا، لَا يُشْرِكُونَ بِاللَّهِ شَيْئًا، إِلَّا شَفَّعَهُمْ اللَّهُ فِيهِ.» رَوَاهُ مُسْلِمٌ.

٢٠١. وَقَالَ: «مَنْ شَهِدَ الجِنَازَةَ حَتَّى يُصَلَّى عَلَيْهَا فَلَهُ قِيرَاطٌ، وَمَنْ شَهِدَهَا حَتَّى تُدْفَنَ فَلَهُ قِيرَاطَانِ. قِيلَ: وَمَا القِيرَاطَانِ؟ قَالَ: مِثْلُ الجَبَلَيْنِ العَظِيمَيْنِ.» مُتَّفَقٌ عَلَيْهِ.

٢٠٢. وَنَهَى النَّبِيُّ ﷺ أَنْ:

١. يُجَصَّصَ القَبْرُ.

٢. وَأَنْ يُقْعَدَ عَلَيْهِ.

٣. وَأَنْ يُبْنَى عَلَيْهِ

203. When the Prophet ﷺ finished burying the deceased, he would stand next to the grave and say, "Seek forgiveness for your brother and ask that he is kept firm, for verily he is being questioned now (by the Angels)." (Abū Dāwūd and authenticated by al Ḥākim.)

204. It is recommended to offer condolences (*Taʿziyah*) to those grieving due to the loss of a person.

205. The Prophet ﷺ cried over a deceased person and said, "Indeed, this is mercy".

206. However, he ﷺ cursed the *nāʾiḥah* (the one who wails) and the *mustamiʿah* (the one who intentionally and attentively listens to the wailing.)

207. The Prophet ﷺ said, "Visit the graves, for it will remind you of the afterlife." (Muslim)

٢٠٣. وَكَانَ إِذَا فَرَغَ مِنْ دَفْنِ المَيِّتِ وَقَفَ عَلَيْه وقال: «اِسْتَغْفِرُوا لِأَخِيكُمْ، وَاسْالوا لَهُ التَّثْبِيتَ، فَإِنَّهُ الآنَ يُسْال.» رَوَاهُ أَبُو دَاوُدَ وصَحَّحَهُ الحَاكِمُ.

٢٠٤. وَيُسْتَحَبُّ تَعْزِيَةُ المصَابِ بِالْمَيِّتِ.

٢٠٥. وَبَكَى النَّبِيُّ ﷺ عَلَى الميّتِ، وَقَالَ: «إِنَّهَا رَحْمَةٌ.»

٢٠٦. مَعَ أَنَّهُ لَعَنَ النَّائِحَةَ وَالْمُسْتَمِعَةَ.

٢٠٧. وَقَالَ: «زُورُوا القُبُورَ فَإِنَّهَا تُذَكِّرُ بِالْآخِرَةِ.» رَوَاهُ مُسْلِمٌ.

208. The one who visits the graves should say:

السَّلامُ عَلَيْكُمْ أَهْلَ دَارِ قَوْمٍ مُؤْمِنِينَ وَإِنَّا إِنْ شَاءَ اللهُ بِكُمْ لاحِقُونَ وَيَرْحَمُ اللهُ الْمُسْتَقْدِمِينَ مِنْكُمْ وَالْمُسْتَأْخِرِينَ نَسْال اللهَ لَنَا ولَكُمْ العَافِيَةَ اللهُمَّ لا تَحْرِمْنَا أَجْرَهُمْ ولا تَفْتِنَّ بَعْدَهُمْ وَاغْفِرْ لَنَا ولَهُمْ نَسْال اللهَ لَنَا وَلَكُمْ العَافِيَةَ

As-Salāmu ʿalaykum ahla dāri qawmin muʾminīn, wa innā in shāʾAllāhu bikum lāḥiqūn. Wa yarḥamullāhu al mustaqdimīn minkum wal mustaʾkhirīn. Nasʾalullāha lana wa lakum al ʿāfiyah. Allāhumma lā taḥrimnā ajrahum wa lā taftinnā baʿdahum waghfir lanā wa lahum, nasʾalullāha lanā wa lakum al ʿāfiyah.

"Peace be upon you, inhabitants of the dwellings who are of the believing community. If Allāh wills, we shall join you. May Allāh have mercy upon those who have gone on ahead of us and those who come later on. We ask Allāh for well-being for us and for you. O Allāh, do not deprive us of their reward and do not put us to trial after them, forgive us and them and we ask Allāh for well-being for us and for you."

209. Any pious deed can be performed with the intention to pass on the reward to the deceased or a living Muslim.

Allāh ﷻ knows best.

٢٠٨. وَيَنْبَغِي لِمَنْ زَارَهَا أَنْ يَقُولَ: «السَّلَامُ عَلَيْكُمْ أَهْلَ دَارِ قَوْمٍ مُؤْمِنِينَ، وَإِنَّا إِنْ شَاءَ اللَّهُ بِكُمْ لَاحِقُونَ، وَيَرْحَمُ اللَّهُ الْمُسْتَقْدِمِينَ مِنْكُمْ وَالْمُسْتَأْخِرِينَ؛ نَسْأَلُ اللَّهَ لَنَا وَلَكُمُ الْعَافِيَةَ اللَّهُمَّ لَا تَحْرِمْنَا أَجْرَهُمْ، وَلَا تَفْتِنَّا بَعْدَهُمْ، وَاغْفِرْ لَنَا وَلَهُمْ، نَسْأَلُ اللَّهَ لَنَا وَلَكُمُ الْعَافِيَةَ.»

٢٠٩. وَأَيُّ قُرْبَةٍ فَعَلَهَا وَجَعَلَ ثَوَابَهَا لِحَيٍّ أَوْ مَيِّتٍ مُسْلِمٍ نَفَعَهُ ذَلِكَ. وَاللَّهُ أَعْلَمُ.

كِتَابُ الزَّكَاة

The Book of Zakāh

210. *Zakāh* is obligatory upon:

1. A Muslim
2. Free person
3. Who possesses the *niṣāb* (the threshold that necessitates *zakāh*)

211. *Zakah* is due on any zakatable wealth only after the passing of a complete lunar year. With the exception of:

1. Agricultural produce
2. An increase to something already above the threshold, like the growth of the *niṣāb,* or profit from trade. In such instances, the year for such growths commences from when the original amount reaches the threshold.

212. *Zakāh* is only due from four types of wealth:

1. Livestock
2. Agricultural produce
3. Monetary assets
4. Merchandise goods

كِتَابُ الزَّكَاةِ

٢١٠. وهِيَ وَاجِبَةٌ على:

١. كُلِّ مسْلِمٍ

٢. حُرٍّ

٣. مَلَكَ نِصَابًا

٢١١. وَلا زَكَاةَ فِي مَالٍ حَتَّى يَحُولَ عَلَيْهِ الحَوْلُ، إلا:

١. الخَارِج مِنْ الأَرْضِ.

٢. ومَا كَانَ تابعًا لِلأَصْلِ، كَنَمَاءِ النِّصَابِ، وَرِبْحِ التِّجَارَةِ، فَإِنَّ حَوْلَهُمَا حَوْلُ أَصْلِهِمَا

٢١٢. وَلا تَجِبُ الزَّكَاةُ إلا فِي أَرْبَعَةِ أَنْوَاعٍ:

١. السَّائِمَة مِنْ بَهِيمَةِ الأَنْعَامِ

٢. والخَارِجِ مِن الأَرْضِ

٣. والأَثْمَان

٤. وَعُرُوضِ التِّجَارَةِ

Zakāh on Grazing Livestock (*sāʾimah*)

213. The basis for the *zakāh* of livestock can be found in the narration of Anas ﷺ in which Abū Bakr ﷺ wrote to him the following,

"The following are the obligations of the alms that the Prophet ﷺ obligated upon the Muslims:

- For twenty-four camels or less, sheep are to be paid as *zakāh*; for every five camels one sheep (*shāh*) is to be paid.
- If there are between twenty-five to thirty-five camels, a *bint makhāḍ* (one-year old female camel) is to be given, and if one is not available then an *ibn labūn* (a male two-year-old camel) is to be given.
- If there are between thirty-six to forty-five (camels), a *bint labūn* (a female two-year-old camel) is to be given
- If there are between forty-six to sixty (camels), one *ḥiqqah* (a female three-year-old camel) is to be given
- If there are between sixty-one to seventy-five (camels), one *jadhaʿah* (a four-year-old camel) is to be given.
- If there are between seventy-six to ninety (camels), two *bint labūn* are to be given.

زَكَاةُ السَّائِمَة

٢١٣. فَأَمَّا السَّائِمَة فَالأَصْلُ فِيهَا حَدِيثُ أَنَسٍ: أَنَّ أَبَا بَكْرٍ رَضِيَ اللهُ عَنْهُ كَتَبَ لَهُ: «هَذِهِ فَرِيضَةُ الصَّدَقَةِ الَّتِي فَرَضَهَا رَسُولُ اللَّه ﷺ عَلَى المُسْلِمِينَ، وَالَّتِي أَمَرَ اللهُ بِهَا رَسُولَهُ:

- فِي أَرْبَعٍ وَعِشْرِينَ مِنَ الإِبِلِ فَمَا دُونَهَا مِنَ الغَنَمِ، فِي كُلِّ خَمْسٍ: شَاةٌ.

- فَإِذَا بَلَغَتْ خَمْسًا وَعِشْرِينَ إِلَى خَمْسٍ وَثَلَاثِينَ، فَفِيهَا: بِنْتُ مَخَاضٍ أُنْثَى، فَإِنْ لَمْ تَكُنْ فَابْنُ لَبُونٍ ذَكَرٍ.

- فَإِذَا بَلَغَتْ سِتًّا وَثَلَاثِينَ إِلَى خَمْسٍ وَأَرْبَعِينَ، فَفِيهَا: بِنْتُ لَبُونٍ أُنْثَى.

- فَإِذَا بَلَغَتْ سِتًّا وَأَرْبَعِينَ إِلَى سِتِّينَ، فَفِيهَا: حِقَّةٌ طَرُوقَةُ الجَمَلِ.

- فَإِذَا بَلَغَتْ وَاحِدًا وَسِتِّينَ إِلَى خَمْسٍ وَسَبْعِينَ، فَفِيهَا: جَذَعَةٌ.

- فَإِذَا بَلَغَتْ سِتًّا وَسَبْعِينَ إِلَى تِسْعِينَ، فَفِيهَا: بِنْتَا لَبُونٍ.

- If there are between ninety-one to one-hundred-and twenty (camels), two *ḥiqqah* are to be given.
- If there are over one-hundred and-twenty (camels), for every forty (over one-hundred-and-twenty) one *bint labūn* is to be given, and for every fifty camels (over one-hundred-and-twenty) one *ḥiqqah* is to be given.
- There is no *zakāh* due from someone who possesses four camels. However, if the owner wants to give something, he can.

Table in summary[5]:

Number of camels	*Zakāh*
5 – 24	1 Sheep for every 5
25 – 35	1 *bint makhāḍ* if unavailable then, 1 *Ibn Labūn*
36 – 45	1 *bint labūn*
46 – 60	1 *ḥiqqah*
61 – 75	1 *jadhaʿah*
76 – 90	two *bint labūn*
91 – 120	2 *ḥiqqah*
121+	1 bint labūn for every 40 and one *ḥiqqah* for every 50

[5] This table and all forthcoming tables have been added by the translator.

- فَإِذَا بَلَغَتْ إِحْدَى وَتِسْعِينَ إِلَى عِشْرِينَ وَمِائَةٍ، فَفِيهَا: حِقَّتَانِ طَرُوقَتَا الجَمَلِ.
- فَإِذَا زَادَتْ عَلَى عِشْرِينَ وَمِائَةٍ، فَفِي كُلِّ أَرْبَعِينَ بِنْتُ لَبُونٍ، وَفِي كُلِّ خَمْسِينَ: حِقَّةٌ.
- وَمَنْ لَمْ يَكُنْ مَعَهُ إِلَّا أَرْبَعٌ مِنْ الإِبِلِ فَلَيْسَ فِيهَا صَدَقَةٌ إِلَّا أَنْ يَشَاءَ رَبُّهَا.

Zakāh on *Ghanam* (sheep & goats)

- If there are between forty and one-hundred-and-twenty sheep, one sheep (*shāh*) is to be given.
- And if there are between one-hundred-and-twenty to two hundred (sheep), two sheep are to be given.
- And if there are between two-hundred to three-hundred (sheep), three sheep are to be given.
- And for over three-hundred sheep, for every extra hundred sheep, one sheep is to be given.
- And if somebody possesses fewer than forty sheep, no *zakāh* is due, but if he wants to give it, he can.
- It is not permissible for different owners of livestock to combine between their respective livestock out of fear of paying more *zakāh.* Likewise, it is not permissible to divide livestock that are already considered as one whole out of fear of paying *zakāh.*
- *Ghanam* that are owned by different owners but graze together (and are looked after by one shepherd etc., only have to give the *zakāh* of one person). However, the value of what is given as *zakāh* has to be shared out amongst the owners.
- It is not permissible to give as *zakāh* that which is old in age, weak and has defects.

وَفِي صَدَقَةِ الغَنَمِ

- فِي سَائِمَتِهَا إِذَا كَانَتْ أَرْبَعِينَ إِلَى عِشْرِينَ وَمِائَةٍ: شَاةٌ.

- فَإِذَا زَادَتْ عَلَى عِشْرِينَ وَمِائَةٍ إِلَى مِائَتَيْنِ، فَفِيهَا شَاتَانِ.

- فَإِذَا زَادَتْ عَلَى مِائَتَيْنِ إِلَى ثَلَاثِمِائَةٍ، فَفِيهَا ثَلَاثُ شِيَاهٍ

- فَإِذَا زَادَتْ عَلَى ثَلَاثِمِائَةٍ، فَفِي كُلِ مِائَةٍ شَاةٌ.

- فَإِذَا كَانَتْ سَائِمَةُ الرَّجُلِ نَاقِصَةً عَنْ أَرْبَعِينَ شَاةً، فَلَيْسَ فِيهَا صَدَقَةٌ إِلَّا أَنْ يَشَاءَ رَبُّهَا

- وَلَا يُجْمَعُ بَيْنَ مُتَفَرِّقٍ، وَلَا يُفَرَّقُ بَيْنَ مُجْتَمِعٍ خَشْيَةَ الصَّدَقَةِ.

- وَمَا كَانَ مِنْ خَلِيطَيْنِ فَإِنَّهُمَا يَتَرَاجَعَانِ بَيْنَهُمَا بِالسَّوِيَّةِ.

- وَلَا يُخْرَجُ فِي الصَّدَقَةِ هَرِمَةً وَلَا ذَاتَ عُوَارٍ.

Table in summary:

Number of sheep	*Zakāh*
40 – 120	1 Sheep
121 – 200	2 sheep
201 - 300	3 sheep
301+ for every hundred	1 additional sheep

- For silver, the *zakāh* is one-fortieth of the total amount (i.e. 2.5%), and if its value is less than two-hundred *dirhams, zakāh* is not required. However, if the owner wants to pay, he can.
- Whoever possesses the amount of camels which obligates the giving of a *jadhaᶜah*, but does not have one, can give a *ḥiqqah* if he has one, and he should include with that two sheep if he can manage that, or give 20 *dirham.*
- And whoever possesses the amount of camels which obligates the giving of a *ḥiqqah,* but does not have one, can give a *jadhaᶜah* instead, and then take in return 20 *dirham* or two sheep from the collector." (Bukhāri)

214. In the narration of Muᶜādh ﷺ it states that, "the Prophet ﷺ commanded him to take from every 30 cows a *tabīᶜ* or a *tabīᶜah* (a one-year-old cow), and from every 40 cows a *musinnah* (a two-year-old cow)". (Abū Dāwūd and Tirmidhi)

- وَفِي الرِّقَةِ فِي مِائَتَيْ دِرْهَمٍ: رُبْعُ العُشْرِ. فَإِنْ لَمْ يَكُنْ إِلَّا تِسْعُونَ وَمِائَةٌ فَلَيْس فِيهَا صَدَقَةٌ، إِلَّا أَنْ يَشَاءَ رَبُّهَا.
- وَمَنْ بَلَغَتْ عِنْدَهُ مِنْ الإِبِلِ صَدَقَةُ الجَذَعَةِ، وَلَيْسَتْ عِنْدَهُ جَذَعَةٌ، وَعِنْدَهُ حِقَّةٌ فَإِنَّهَا تُقْبَلُ مِنْهُ الحِقَّةُ، وَيُجْعَلُ مَعَهَا شَاتَانِ إِنْ اِسْتَيْسَرَتَا لَهُ، أَوْ عِشْرُونَ دِرْهَمًا.
- وَمَنْ بَلَغَتْ عِنْدَهُ صَدَقَةُ الحِقَّةِ وَلَيْسَتْ عِنْدَهُ الحِقَّةُ، وَعِنْدَهُ الجَذَعَةُ فَإِنَّهَا تُقْبَلُ مِنْهُ الجَذَعَةُ، وَيُعْطِيهِ المصدِّقُ عِشْرِينَ دِرْهَمًا أَوْ شَاتَيْنِ.» رَوَاهُ البُخَارِيُّ.

٢١٤. وَفِي حَدِيثِ مُعَاذٍ: أَنَّ النَّبِيَّ صَلّى اللهُ عَليه وسلَّم أَمَرَهُ أَنْ يَأْخُذَ مِنْ كُلِّ ثَلَاثِينَ بَقَرَةً: تَبِيعًا أَوْ تَبِيعَةً وَمِنْ كُلِّ أَرْبَعِينَ: مُسِنَّةً. رَوَاهُ أَهْلُ السُّنَنِ

215. *Zakāh* of *athmān* (Monetary assets):

It has preceded that there is no *zakāh* on monetary assets until it reaches 200 *dirham,* of which 2.5% has to be given as *zakāh.*

216. *Zakāh* of agricultural produce of grains and fruits:

The Prophet said ﷺ, "There is no *ṣadaqah* (i.e. *zakāh*) on dates if they are fewer than five *awsuq.*" (Agreed upon)

A *Wasq* (pl = *awsuq*) is equivalent to 60 *ṣāʿ*. Therefore, the *niṣāb* for grains and fruits is 300 *ṣāʿ*, according to the *ṣāʿ* used at the time of the Prophet ﷺ.

217. He ﷺ also said, "On a land irrigated by rainwater or by natural water channels or if the land is wet due to a nearby water channel, *ʿushr* (i.e. one-tenth) is compulsory (as *zakāh*); and on land irrigated by a well, half of an *ʿushr* (i.e. one-twentieth) is compulsory (as *zakāh* on the yield of the land)." (Bukhāri)

218. Sahl bin Abī Ḥathmah said, "The Messenger of Allāh ﷺ commanded us that 'when you make an assessment, then take it and leave a third; if you do not leave a third, then leave a quarter.'" (Abū Dāwūd & Tirmidhi)

٢١٥. وَأَمَّا صَدَقَةُ الأَثْمَانِ

فَقَدْ تَقَدَّمَ أَنَّهُ لَيْسَ فِيهَا شَيْءٌ حَتَّى تَبْلُغَ مِائَتَيْ دِرْهَمٍ، وَفِيهَا رُبْعُ العُشْرِ.

٢١٦. وَأَمَّا صَدَقَةُ الخَارِجِ مِنْ الأَرْضِ مِنْ الحُبُوبِ وَالثِّمَارِ فَقَدْ قَالَ النَّبِيُّ ﷺ: «لَيْسَ فِيمَا دُونَ خَمْسَةِ أَوْسُقٍ مِنْ التَّمْرِ صَدَقَةٌ.» مُتَّفَقٌ عَلَيْهِ.

وَالْوَسْقُ: سِتُّونَ صَاعًا، فَيَكُونُ النِّصَابُ لِلْحُبُوبِ وَالثِّمَارِ: ثَلَاثُمِائَةِ صَاعٍ بِصَاعِ النَّبِيِّ ﷺ.

٢١٧. وَقَالَ النَّبِيُّ ﷺ: فِيمَا سَقَتْ السَّمَاءُ وَالْعُيُونُ، أَوْ كَانَ عَثَرِيًّا: «العُشْرُ، وَفِيمَا سُقِيَ بِالنَّضْحِ: نِصْفُ العُشْرِ.» رَوَاهُ البُخَارِيُّ.

٢١٨. وَعَنْ سَهْلِ بْنِ أَبِي حَثْمَةَ قَالَ: «أَمَرَنَا رَسُولُ اللَّهِ ﷺ: إِذَا خَرَصْتُمْ فَخُذُوا وَدَعُوا الثُّلُثَ، فَإِنْ لَمْ تَدَعُوا الثُّلُثَ فَدَعُوا الربع.» رَوَاهُ أَهْلُ السُّنَنِ.

219. *Zakāh* on merchandise goods i.e. that which has been prepared for buying and selling in order to gain profit:

220. It should be valued after a year according to what will benefit the Muslims the most, and then give what is due in gold or silver.

221. 2.5% of the value should be given in *zakāh.*

222. A creditor who does not expect to see his money repaid, either because the debtor is *mumāṭil* (keeps deferring the payment even though is capable of settling the debt) or is *muʿsir* (a person who cannot afford to pay back the creditor) does not have to pay *zakāh* on the value of the debt.

223. Otherwise, he has to pay *zakāh* on it.

224. It is obligatory to give *zakāh* from the average quality of his wealth.

225. It is not adequate enough to give it from the lowest quality of his wealth.

226. It is not a must that a person gives it with the best quality of his wealth unless he chooses to do so.

زَكَاةَ عُرُوضِ التِّجَارَةِ

٢١٩. وَأَمَّا عُرُوضُ التِّجَارَةِ: وَهُوَ كُلُّ مَا أُعِدَّ لِلْبَيْعِ وَالشِّرَاءِ لِأَجْلِ الرِّبْحِ.

٢٢٠. فَإِنَّهُ يُقَوَّمُ إِذَا حَالَ الحَوْلُ بِالْأَحَظِّ لِلْمَسَاكِينِ مِنْ ذَهَبٍ أَوْ فِضَّةٍ.

٢٢١. وَيَجِبُ فِيهِ رُبْعُ العُشْرِ.

٢٢٢. وَمَنْ كَانَ لَهُ دَيْنٌ وَمَالٌ لَا يَرْجُو وُجُودَهُ، كَالذِي عَلَى مُمَاطِلٍ أَوْ مُعْسِرٍ لَا وَفَاءَ لَهُ: فَلَا زَكَاةَ فِيهِ.

٢٢٣. وَإِلَّا فَفِيهِ الزَّكَاةُ.

٢٢٤. وَيَجِبُ الإِخْرَاجُ مِنْ وَسَطِ المَالِ.

٢٢٥. وَلَا يُجْزِئُ مِنَ الأَدْوَنِ.

٢٢٦. وَلَا يَلْزَمُ الخِيَارُ إِلَّا أَنْ يَشَاءَ رَبُّهُ.

227. Abū Hurayrah رضي الله عنه narrated that the Prophet ﷺ said, "There is *khumus* (i.e. a fifth) due on *Rikāz* (buried treasure and precious minerals)" (Agreed upon)

٢٢٧. وَفِي حَدِيثِ أَبِي هُرَيْرَةَ مَرْفُوعًا: «فِي الرِّكَازِ الخُمُسُ.»
مُتَّفَقٌ عَلَيْهِ

بَابُ زَكَاةِ الفِطْر

Chapter: *Zakāh al Fiṭr*

228. Ibn ᶜUmar ﵄ narrated that the Prophet ﷺ "obligated *zakāh al fiṭr* by giving a *ṣāᶜ* in dates or a *ṣāᶜ* in barley. It was obligated upon the slave, the free, men, women, young and old from the Muslims. He ﷺ ordered that it should be given before people leave for the prayer." (Agreed upon)

229. It is obligatory:

- For oneself, and for those whom he cares for.
- If one had more than a day and night's worth of sustenance.
- To give a *ṣāᶜ* of dates or barley or cottage cheese or sultanas or wheat.

230. It is better to give (from the above) that which is more beneficial to the poor.

231. It is not permissible to delay the giving of the *zakāh* after the day of *ᶜĪd.*

بَابُ زَكَاةِ الفِطْرِ

٢٢٨. عَنْ ابْنِ عُمَرَ قَالَ: فَرَضَ رَسُولُ اللّٰهِ ﷺ زَكَاةَ الفِطْرِ: صَاعًا مِنْ تَمْرٍ، أَوْ صَاعًا مِنْ شَعِيرٍ، عَلَى العَبْدِ وَالْحُرِّ، وَالذَّكَرِ وَالْأُنْثَى، وَالصَّغِيرِ وَالْكَبِيرِ مِنْ المسْلِمِينَ. وَأُمِرَ بِهَا أَنْ تُؤَدَّى قَبْلَ خُرُوجِ النَّاسِ إِلَى الصَّلَاةِ. مُتَّفَقٌ عَلَيْهِ.

٢٢٩. وَتَجِبُ:

١. لِنَفْسِهِ، وَلِمَنْ تَلْزَمُهُ مُؤْنَتُهُ.

٢. إِذَا كَانَ ذَلِكَ فَاضِلًا عَنْ قُوتِ يَوْمِهِ وَلَيْلَتِهِ.

٣. صَاعٌ مِنْ تَمْرٍ أَوْ شَعِيرٍ أَوْ أَقِطٍ أَوْ زَبِيبٍ أَوْ بُرٍّ.

٢٣٠. وَالْأَفْضَلُ فِيهَا: الأَنْفَعُ.

٢٣١. وَلَا يَحِلُّ تَأْخِيرُهَا عَنْ يَوْمِ العِيدِ

232. The Prophet ﷺ obligated it upon those who fasted to purify them from the foul speech and obscenity and also to feed the poor.

- Whoever gives the charity before the prayer will have it accepted from him (as *zakāh al fiṭr*).
- However, if one gives the charity after the prayer then it will be considered to be a normal act of charity (i.e. *ṣadaqah,* but not *zakāh ul fiṭr*). (Abū Dāwūd & ibn Mājah).

233. The Prophet ﷺ said, "Seven people will be shaded by Allāh ﷾ under His shade on the day when there will be no shade but His. They are: A just ruler, a young man who has been brought up worshipping Allāh (alone), sincerely, from childhood, a man whose heart is attached to the mosque, two people who love each other only for Allāh's ﷾ sake and they meet and part in Allāh's cause only, a man who refuses the call of a charming woman of beauty and position for illegal sexual intercourse with her, and says, "I fear Allāh", a person who practises charity so secretly that his left hand does not know what his right hand has given and a man who remembered Allāh ﷾ in private and so his eyes shed tears." (Agreed upon)

٢٣٢. وَقَدْ فَرَضَهَا رَسُولُ اللَّهِ صلى الله عليه وسلم طُهْرَةً لِلصَّائِمِ مِنْ اللَّغْوِ وَالرَّفَثِ، وَطُعْمَةً لِلمَسَاكِينَ.

- فَمَنْ أَدَّاهَا قَبْلَ الصَّلاةِ فَهِيَ زكاةٌ مَقْبُولَة.
- ومَنْ أَدَّاهَا بَعْدَ الصَّلاةِ فَهِيَ صَدَقَةٌ مِن الصَّدَقَات.

رَوَاهُ أَبُو دَاوُد وَابْنُ مَاجَهْ

٢٣٣. وَقَالَ ﷺ: «سَبْعَةٌ يُظِلُّهُمْ اللَّهُ فِي ظِلِّهِ، يَوْمَ لَا ظِلَّ إِلَّا ظِلُّهُ: إِمَامٌ عَادِلٌ، وَشَابٌّ نَشَأَ فِي طَاعَةِ اللَّهِ، وَرَجُلٌ قَلْبُهُ مُعَلَّقٌ بِالْمَسَاجِدِ، وَرَجُلَانِ تَحَابَّا فِي اللَّهِ، اِجْتَمَعَا عَلَيْهِ وَتَفَرَّقَا عَلَيْهِ، وَرَجُلٌ دَعَتْهُ اِمْرَأَةٌ ذَاتُ مَنْصِبٍ وَجَمَالٍ، فَقَالَ: إِنِّي أَخَافُ اللَّهَ، وَرَجُلٌ تَصَدَّقَ بِصَدَقَةٍ فَأَخْفَاهَا حَتَّى لَا تَعْلَمَ شِمَالُهُ مَا تُنْفِقُ يَمِينُهُ، وَرَجُلٌ ذَكَرَ اللهَ خَالِيًا فَفَاضَتْ عَيْنَاهُ.»

مُتَّفَقٌ عَلَيْهِ

بَابُ أَهْلِ الزَّكَاة وَمَنْ تُدْفَعُ لَه

Chapter: The Recipients of *Zakāh*

234. *Zakāh* is not given to anyone except the eight categories that Allāh ﷻ mentions in the Qurʾān,

"*Alms are meant only for the poor, the needy, those who administer them, those whose hearts need winning over, to free slaves and help those in debt, for God's cause, and for travellers in need. This is ordained by God; God is all knowing and wise.*" (9:60)

235. It is permissible to give one's *zakāh* to only one of the categories, due to the statement of the Prophet ﷺ to Muʿādh رضي الله عنه, "And if they respond to you in that, then make them aware that Allāh ﷻ has obligated upon them a charity that is taken from their rich and given to their poor." (Agreed upon)

236. It is not permissible to give the *zakāh* to:

- A wealthy person.
- A person who is strong and able to earn his living.
- The family of the Prophet ﷺ i.e. Banū Hāshim and their freed slaves.
- A person who one is already responsible for providing for.
- A disbeliever.

بَابُ أَهْلِ الزَّكَاةِ وَمَنْ تُدْفَعُ لَهُ

٢٣٤. لَا تُدْفَعُ الزَّكَاةُ إِلَّا لِلْأَصْنَافِ الثَّمَانِيَةِ الذِينَ ذَكَرَهُمْ اللَّهُ بِقَوْلِهِ: ﴿إِنَّمَا ٱلصَّدَقَٰتُ لِلْفُقَرَآءِ وَٱلْمَسَٰكِينِ وَٱلْعَٰمِلِينَ عَلَيْهَا وَٱلْمُؤَلَّفَةِ قُلُوبُهُمْ وَفِى ٱلرِّقَابِ وَٱلْغَٰرِمِينَ وَفِى سَبِيلِ ٱللَّهِ وَٱبْنِ ٱلسَّبِيلِ ۖ فَرِيضَةً مِّنَ ٱللَّهِ ۗ وَٱللَّهُ عَلِيمٌ حَكِيمٌ﴾ [التَّوْبَة: ٦٠]

٢٣٥. وَيَجُوزُ الاقْتِصَارُ عَلَى وَاحِدٍ مِنْهُمْ لِقَوْلِهِ ﷺ لِمُعَاذٍ «فَإِنْ هُمْ أَطَاعُوكَ لِذَلِكَ فَأَعْلِمْهُمْ: أَنَّ اللَّهَ افْتَرَضَ عَلَيْهِمْ صَدَقَةً تُؤْخَذُ مِنْ أَغْنِيَائِهِمْ فَتُرَدَّ عَلَى فُقَرَائِهِمْ.» مُتَّفَقٌ عَلَيْهِ

٢٣٦. وَلَا تَحِلُّ الزَّكَاةُ:

- لِغَنِيٍّ
- وَلَا لِقَوِيٍّ مُكْتَسِبٍ
- وَلَا لِآلِ مُحَمَّدٍ، وَهُمْ بَنُو هَاشِمٍ وَمَوَالِيهِمْ
- وَلَا لِمَنْ تَجِبُ عَلَيْهِ نَفَقَتُهُ حَالَ جَرَيَانِهَا
- وَلَا لِكَافِرٍ.

237. However, it is permissible to give supererogatory acts of charity to the above groups.

238. Nonetheless, to give to a category that is in more need is more befitting.

239. The Prophet said ﷺ, "Whoever asks the people for money in order to amass more wealth is asking for a burning coal, so let him ask for less or more." (Muslim)

240. The Prophet ﷺ said to ʿUmar ؓ once, "Whatever of this wealth comes to you when you were not wishing for it or asking for it, then take it, otherwise do not wish for it." (Muslim)

٢٣٧. فَأَمَّا صَدَقَةُ التَّطَوُّعِ فَيَجُوزُ دَفْعُهَا إِلَى هَؤُلَاءِ وَغَيْرِهِمْ.

٢٣٨.وَلَكِنْ كُلَّمَا كَانَتْ أَنْفَعَ نَفْعًا عَامًّا أَوْ خَاصًّا فَهِيَ أَكْمَلُ.

٢٣٩. وَقَالَ النَّبِيُّ ﷺ:«مَنْ سَالَ النَّاسَ أَمْوَالَهُمْ تَكَثُّرًا فَإِنَّمَا يَسْال جَمْرًا، فَلْيَسْتَقِلَّ أَوْ لِيَسْتَكْثِرْ.» رَوَاهُ مُسْلِمٌ.

٢٤٠. وَقَالَ ﷺ لِعُمَرَ: «مَا جَاءَكَ مِنْ هَذَا المَالِ وَأَنْتَ غَيْرُ مُشْرِفٍ وَلَا سَائِلٍ فَخُذْهُ، وَمَا لَا فَلَا تُتْبِعْهُ نَفْسَكَ.» رَوَاهُ مُسْلِمٌ

كِتَابُ الصِّيَام

The Book of Fasting

241. The command to fast is based upon the following verse,

"O You who believe! Fasting has been prescribed upon you like it was prescribed upon those who came before you so that you may be mindful of God." (2:183)

242. Fasting in the month of Ramaḍān is obligatory upon every:

1. Muslim
2. Mature person
3. Sane person
4. Person capable of fasting

It becomes obligatory to fast if the crescent is sighted or by completing Shaᶜbān as 30 days.

The Prophet ﷺ said, "When you see the crescent (of Ramaḍān), start fasting, and when you see the crescent (of Shawwāl), stop fasting; and if the sky is overcast, calculate when it should appear." (Agreed upon) In another narration it states, "...then count it as 30 days." And in another narration, it states, "...complete Shaᶜbān as thirty days." (Bukhāri)

كِتَابُ الصِّيَامِ

٢٤١. الأَصْلُ فِيهِ قَوْلُهُ تَعَالَى: ﴿يَٰٓأَيُّهَا ٱلَّذِينَ ءَامَنُواْ كُتِبَ عَلَيْكُمُ ٱلصِّيَامُ كَمَا كُتِبَ عَلَى ٱلَّذِينَ مِن قَبْلِكُمْ لَعَلَّكُمْ تَتَّقُونَ ﴿١٨٣﴾﴾ [البقرة: ١٨٣]

٢٤٢. وَيَجِبُ صِيَامُ رَمَضَانَ عَلَى كُلِّ:

١. مُسْلِمٍ

٢. بَالِغٍ

٣. عَاقِلٍ

٤. قَادِرٍ عَلَى الصَّوْمِ

٥. بِرُؤْيَةِ هِلَالِهِ، أَوْ إِكْمَالِ شَعْبَانَ ثَلَاثِينَ يَوْمًا

قَالَ صَلَّى اللهُ عَلَيْهِ وَسَلَّمَ: «إِذَا رَأَيْتُمُوهُ فَصُومُوا، وَإِذَا رَأَيْتُمُوهُ فَأَفْطِرُوا، فَإِنْ غُمَّ عَلَيْكُمْ فَاقْدُرُوا لَهُ.» مُتَّفَقٌ عَلَيْهِ. وَفِي لفظٍ: «فَاقْدُرُوا لَهُ ثَلَاثِينَ» وَفِي لَفْظٍ: «فَأَكْمِلُوا عِدَّةَ شَعْبَانَ ثَلَاثِينَ.» رَوَاهُ البُخَارِيُّ

243. The beginning of Ramaḍān can be determined by the testimony of a single and just individual. As for the remaining months of the year, two just witnesses are required to establish the beginning of the month.

244. It is obligatory to make the intention for the obligatory fast the night before the fast begins.

245. As for the recommended fast, the intention can be made during the day of the fast itself.

246. The sick who will be harmed by fasting, in addition to the traveller, can opt to fast or not.

247. It is prohibited for the menstruating woman and a woman who has post-natal bleeding to fast. However, they have to make up the fasts they missed (*qaḍāʾ*).

248. If a pregnant woman or a woman who breastfeeds fears for their child, they should break their fast, make it up and feed a poor person for every day that they missed.

249. As for the person who is unable to fast due to old age or has an illness that one does not expect to be cured from, they should feed a poor person (*miskīn*) for every day missed.

٢٤٣. وَيُصَامُ بِرُؤْيَةِ عَدْلٍ لِهِلَالِهِ وَلَا يُقْبَلُ فِي بَقِيَّةِ الشُّهُورِ إِلَّا عَدْلَانِ.

٢٤٤. وَيَجِبُ تَبْيِيتُ النِّيَّةِ لِصِيَامِ الفَرْضِ

٢٤٥. وَأَمَّا النَّفْلُ: فَيَجُوزُ بِنِيَّةٍ مِنَ النَّهَارِ.

٢٤٦. وَالْمَرِيضُ الذِي يَتَضَرَّرُ بِالصَّوْمِ وَالْمُسَافِرُ لَهُمَا الفِطْرُ وَالصِّيَامُ.

٢٤٧. وَالْحَائِضُ وَالنُّفَسَاءُ يَحْرُمُ عَلَيْهِمَا الصِّيَامُ، وَعَلَيْهِمَا القَضَاءُ.

٢٤٨. وَالحَامِلُ وَالمرْضِعُ إِذَا خَافَتَا عَلَى وَلَدَيْهِمَا، أَفْطَرَتَا، وقَضَتَا، وَأَطْعَمَتَا عَنْ كُلِّ يَوْمٍ مِسْكِينًا

٢٤٩. وَالعَاجِزُ عَنْ الصَّوْمِ، لِكِبَرٍ أَوْ مَرَضٍ لا يُرْجَى بُرْؤُهُ، فَإِنَّهُ يُطْعِمُ عَنْ كُلِّ يَوْمٍ مِسْكِينًا

250. Whoever intentionally broke their fast (without a valid reason) only has to make it up (*qaḍāʾ*) if it was due to eating, drinking, intentionally vomiting, cupping or ejaculation due to fondling.

251. However, if one broke their fast due to sexual intercourse, then they have to make up the fast and free a slave. If one cannot find a slave to free, they have to fast two consecutive months. If one cannot do that, they have to feed 60 poor people.

252. The Prophet ﷺ said, "Whoever was fasting and ate or drank out of forgetfulness should complete his fast, for verily it was Allāh ﷻ who nourished him with the food and drink." (Agreed upon)

253. He ﷺ also said, "Mankind will remain to be in a good state on condition they hasten to break their fast." (Agreed upon)

254. He ﷺ also said, "Take the *suḥūr,* for verily there is blessing in it." (Agreed upon)

255. He ﷺ also said, "If one of you breaks his fast, then let him break it with a date. If he does not find one, then let him break it with water, for verily it is pure." (Abū Dāwūd & Tirmidhi)

٢٥٠. وَمَنْ أَفْطَرَ فَعَلَيْهِ القَضَاءُ فَقَطْ، إِذَا كَانَ فِطْرُهُ بِأَكْلٍ، أَوْ بِشُرْبٍ، أَوْ قَيْءٍ عَمْدًا، أَوْ حِجَامَةٍ، أَوْ إِمْنَاءٍ بِمبَاشَرَةٍ

٢٥١. إِلا مَنْ أَفْطَرَ بِجمَاعٍ فَإِنَّهُ يَقْضِي وَيَعْتِقُ رَقَبَةً، فَإِنْ لَمْ يَجِدْ فَصِيَامُ شَهْرَيْنِ مُتَتَابِعَيْنِ، فَإِنْ لَمْ يَسْتَطِعْ فَإِطْعَامُ سِتِّينَ مِسْكِينًا

٢٥٢. وَقَالَ النَّبِيُّ ﷺ «مَنْ نَسِيَ وَهُوَ صَائِمٌ فَأَكَلَ أَوْ شَرِبَ فَلْيُتِمَّ صَوْمَهُ، فَإِنَّمَا أَطْعَمَهُ اللَّهُ وَسَقَاهُ.» مُتَّفَقٌ عَلَيْهِ.

٢٥٣. وَقَالَ ﷺ: «لَا يَزَالُ النَّاسُ بِخَيْرٍ مَا عَجَّلُوا الفِطْرَ.» مُتَّفَقٌ عَلَيْهِ.

٢٥٤. وَقَالَ ﷺ: «تَسَحَّرُوا، فَإِنَّ فِي السُّحُورِ بَرَكَةً.» مُتَّفَقٌ عَلَيْهِ

٢٥٥. وَقَالَ ﷺ: «إِذَا أَفْطَرَ أَحَدُكُمْ فَلْيُفْطِرْ عَلَى تَمْرٍ، فَإِنْ لَمْ يَجِدْ فَلْيُفْطِرْ عَلَى مَاءٍ، فَإِنَّهُ طَهُورٌ.» رَوَاهُ الخَمْسَةُ

256. He ﷺ also said, "Whoever does not give up false speech and acting according to it, and ignorant conduct, Allāh ﷻ has no need of him giving up his food and drink." (Bukhāri)

257. He ﷺ also said, "Whoever dies owing fasts, his heir should fast on his behalf." (Agreed upon)

258. The Prophet ﷺ was asked about fasting on the day of *ʿArafah,* to which he ﷺ replied, "It erases the sins of the past year and the remaining."

259. He ﷺ was also asked about fasting on the day of *ʿĀshūrāʾ*, to which he ﷺ replied, "It erases the sins of the past year."

260. He ﷺ was also asked about fasting on Mondays, to which he ﷺ replied, "That was the day in which I was born, the day I was sent as a messenger or the day revelation descended upon me." (Muslim)

261. He ﷺ also said, "Whoever fasted in Ramaḍān and followed it up with six fasts in *Shawwāl* will be rewarded as if he fasted for the whole year." (Muslim)

262. Abu Dharr رضي الله عنه said, "The Prophet ﷺ commanded us to fast three days of each month; the 13th, 14th and 15th." (Nasāʾi and Tirmidhi)

٢٥٦. وَقَالَ ﷺ: «مَنْ لَمْ يَدَعْ قَوْلَ الزُّورِ وَالْعَمَلَ بِهِ وَالْجَهْلَ فَلَيْسَ لِلَّهِ حَاجَةٌ فِي أَنْ يَدَعَ طَعَامَهُ وَشَرَابَهُ.» رَوَاهُ الْبُخَارِيُّ.

٢٥٧. وَقَالَ ﷺ: «مَنْ مَاتَ وَعَلَيْهِ صِيَامٌ صَامَ عَنْهُ وَلِيُّهُ.» مُتَّفَقٌ عَلَيْهِ.

٢٥٨. وَسُئِلَ عَنْ صَوْمِ يَوْمِ عَرَفَةَ فَقَالَ ﷺ: «يُكَفِّرُ السَّنَةَ الْمَاضِيَةَ، وَالْبَاقِيَةَ.»

٢٥٩. وَسُئِلَ عَنْ صِيَامِ عَاشُورَاءَ فَقَالَ ﷺ: «يُكَفِّرُ السَّنَةَ الْمَاضِيَةَ.»

٢٦٠. وَسُئِلَ عَنْ صَوْمِ يَوْمِ الاثْنَيْنِ فَقَالَ ﷺ: «ذَاكَ يَوْمٌ وُلِدْتُ فِيهِ، وَبُعِثْتُ فِيهِ، أَوْ أُنْزِلَ عَلَيَّ فِيهِ.» رَوَاهُ مُسْلِمٌ.

٢٦١. وقال ﷺ «مَنْ صَامَ رَمَضَانَ، ثُمَّ أَتْبَعَهُ سِتًّا مِنْ شَوَّالَ، كَانَ كَصِيَامِ الدَّهْرِ.» رَوَاهُ مُسْلِمٌ

٢٦٢. وَقَالَ أَبُو ذَرٍّ: «أَمَرَنَا رَسُولُ اللَّهِ ﷺ أَنْ نَصُومَ مِنَ الشَّهْرِ ثَلَاثَةَ أَيَّامٍ ثَلَاثَ عَشْرَةَ، وَأَرْبَعَ عَشْرَةَ، وَخَمْسَ عَشْرَةَ.» رَوَاهُ النَّسَائِيُّ وَالتِّرْمِذِيُّ

263. The Prophet ﷺ forbade to fast on two days: *ʿĪd al Fiṭr* and *ʿĪd al Aḍhā.* (Agreed upon)

264. He ﷺ also said, "The days of *Tashrīq* are days of eating, drinking and remembering Allāh ﷻ." (Muslim)

265. He ﷺ also said, "Do not fast on *Jumuʿah,* unless you fast the day before it or the day after it." (Agreed upon)

266. He ﷺ also said, "Whoever fasts in the month of Ramaḍān with *Īmān* and with hope of reward will be forgiven for their previous sins. And whoever stands in the Night of Decree in prayer with *Īmān* and hope of reward will be forgiven for their previous sins." (Agreed upon)

267. The Prophet ﷺ used to practice *Iʿtikāf* (spiritual retreat) during the last ten days of Ramaḍān until he passed away. His wives used to observe *Iʿtikāf* after that. (Agreed upon)

268. He ﷺ also said, "Do not travel to a place for the purpose of worship except three places: *al Masjid Al Ḥarām,* my mosque and *al Masjid al Aqṣā.*" (Agreed upon)

٢٦٣. وَنَهَى عَنْ صِيَامِ يَوْمَيْنِ: يَوْمِ الفِطْرِ، وَيَوْمِ النَّحْرِ. مُتَّفَقٌ عَلَيْهِ.

٢٦٤. وَقَالَ ﷺ: «أَيَّامُ التَّشْرِيقِ: أَيَّامُ أَكْلٍ وَشُرْبٍ وَذِكْرٌ لِلَّهِ عَزَّوَجَلَّ». رَوَاهُ مُسْلِم.

٢٦٥. وَقَالَ ﷺ: «لَا يَصُومَنَّ أَحَدُكُمْ يَوْمَ الجُمْعَةِ، إِلَّا أَنْ يَصُومَ يَوْمًا قَبْلَهُ أَوْ يَوْمًا بَعْدَهُ.» مُتَّفَقٌ عَلَيْهِ.

٢٦٦. وَقَالَ ﷺ: «مَنْ صَامَ رَمَضَانَ إِيمانًا وَاحْتِسَابًا غُفِرَ لَهُ مَا تَقَدَّمَ مِنْ ذَنْبِهِ، وَمَنْ قَامَ لَيْلَةَ القَدْرِ إِيمانًا وَاحْتِسَابًا غُفِرَ لَهُ مَا تَقَدَّمَ مِنْ ذَنْبِهِ.» مُتَّفَقٌ عَلَيْهِ

٢٦٧. وَكَانَ ﷺ يَعْتَكِفُ العَشْرَ الأَوَاخِرَ مِنْ رَمَضَانَ حَتَّى تَوَفَّاهُ اللَّهُ، وَاعْتَكَفَ أَزْوَاجُهُ مِنْ بَعْدِهِ. مُتَّفَقٌ عَلَيْهِ.

٢٦٨. وَقَالَ ﷺ: «لَا تُشَدُّ الرِّحَالُ إِلَّا إِلَى ثَلَاثَةِ مَسَاجِدَ: المسْجِدِ الحَرَامِ، وَمَسْجِدِي هَذَا، وَالْمَسْجِدِ الأَقْصَى.» مُتَّفَقٌ عَلَيْهِ

كِتَابُ الْحَجِّ

The Book of *Ḥajj*

269. The command to perform the pilgrimage is derived from the saying of Allāh ﷻ,

"Pilgrimage to the House is a duty owed to God by people who are able to undertake it. Those who reject this [should know that] God has no need of anyone." (3:97)

270. Having the ability to go (*istiṭāʿah*) is the greatest condition for it. It is defined as possessing the provisions and means of transport necessary to undertake the journey, in addition to having the basic provisions for living.

271. For a woman to be accompanied by a *maḥram* (close male relative) falls under *istiṭāʿah* as well, if she needs to travel.

272. The ḥadīth of Jābir ؓ regarding the *Ḥajj* of the Prophet ﷺ contains the most important rulings of *Ḥajj*. The narration was reported by Muslim that,

كِتَابُ الحَجِّ

٢٦٩. وَالأَصْلُ فِيهِ قَوْلُهُ تَعَالَى: ﴿وَلِلَّهِ عَلَى ٱلنَّاسِ حِجُّ ٱلْبَيْتِ مَنِ ٱسْتَطَاعَ إِلَيْهِ سَبِيلًاۚ﴾ [آل عِمْرَان: ٩٧]

٢٧٠. وَالِاسْتِطَاعَةُ: أَعْظَمُ شُرُوطِهِ، وَهِيَ: مِلْكُ الزَّادِ وَالرَّاحِلَةِ، بَعْدَ ضَرُورَاتِ الإِنْسَانِ وَحَوَائِجِهِ الأَصْلِيَّةِ.

٢٧١. وَمِنْ الاسْتِطَاعَةِ: أَنْ يَكُونَ لِلْمَرْأَةِ مَحْرَمٌ إِذَا احْتَاجَ لِسَفَرٍ.

٢٧٢. وَحَدِيثُ جَابِرٍ فِي حَجِّ النَّبِيِّ ﷺ يَشْتَمِلُ عَلَى أَعْظَمِ أَحْكَامِ الحَجِّ، وَهُوَ مَا رَوَاهُ مُسْلِمٌ عَنْ جَابِرِ بْنِ عَبْدِ اللَّهِ رَضِيَ اللَّهُ عَنْهُمَا:

1. "The Messenger of Allāh ﷺ stayed in Medina for nine years but did not perform *Ḥajj*, then he made a public announcement in the tenth year to the effect that Allāh's Messenger ﷺ was about to perform the *Ḥajj*. A large number of people came to Madīnah and all of them were anxious to follow the Messenger of Allāh ﷺ.
2. We set out with him ﷺ till we reached Dhul-Ḥulaifa. Asmāʾ, daughter of Umais رضي الله عنها gave birth to Muḥammad ibn Abi Bakr. She sent a message to the Messenger of Allāh ﷺ asking him, "What should I do?" He ﷺ replied, "Take a bath, bandage your private parts and enter the state of *iḥrām*.
3. The Messenger of Allāh ﷺ then prayed in the mosque and then mounted al-Qaṣwāʾ (his she-camel) and it stood erect with him on its back at al-Baidāʾ. He ﷺ pronounced the Oneness of Allāh سبحانه وتعالى (saying),

لَبَّيْكَ اللَّهُمَّ لَبَّيْكَ لَبَّيْكَ لاَ شَرِيكَ لَكَ لَبَّيْكَ إِنَّ الْحَمْدَ وَالنِّعْمَةَ لَكَ وَالْمُلْكَ لاَ شَرِيكَ لَكَ

Labbaik Allāhumma labbaik, labbaika Lā sharīka laka labbayk, innal ḥamda wan-Niʿmata laka wal mulk, lā sharīka lak.

١. أَنَّ النَّبِيَّ ﷺ مَكَثَ فِي المدِينَةِ تِسْعَ سِنِينَ لَمْ يَحُجَّ، ثُمَّ أَذَّنَ فِي النَّاسِ فِي العَاشِرَةِ: أَنَّ رَسُولَ اللَّهِ حَاجٌّ، فَقَدِمَ المدِينَةَ بَشَرٌ كَثِيرٌ كُلُّهُمْ يَلْتَمِسُ أَنْ يَأْتَمَّ بِرَسُولِ اللَّهِ ﷺ ، وَيَعْمَلُ مِثْلَهُ.

٢. فَخَرَجْنَا مَعَهُ حَتَّى إِذَا أَتَيْنَا ذَا الْحُلَيْفَةِ، فَوَلَدَتْ أَسْمَاءُ بِنْتُ عُمَيْسٍ مُحَمَّدَ بْنَ أَبِي بَكْرٍ، فَأَرْسَلَتْ إِلَى رَسُولِ اللَّهِ ﷺ : كَيْفَ أَصْنَعُ؟ قَالَ: اِغْتَسِلِي، وَاسْتَثْفِرِي بِثَوْبٍ، وَأَحْرِمِي.

٣. فَصَلَّى رَسُولُ اللَّهِ -صَلَّى اللَّهُ عَلَيْهِ وَسَلَّمَ فِي المسْجِدِ ثُمَّ رَكِبَ القَصْوَاءَ حَتَّى إِذَا اِسْتَوَتْ بِهِ نَاقَتُهُ عَلَى البَيْدَاءِ أَهَلَّ بِالتَّوْحِيدِ: «لَبَّيْكَ اللَّهُمَّ لَبَّيْكَ، لَبَّيْكَ لَا شَرِيكَ لَكَ لَبَّيْكَ، إِنَّ الحَمْدَ وَالنِّعْمَةَ لَكَ وَالْمُلْكَ، لَا شَرِيكَ لَكَ».

"I respond to Your call O Allah! I respond to Your call, You have no partner, I respond to Your call. All praise, thanks and blessings are for You. And You have no partners with You."

4. The people also raised their voices in *talbiyah* which they used to utter, but the Messenger of Allāh ﷺ did not reject or oppose what they did.
5. The Messenger of Allāh ﷺ adhered to his own *talbiyah.*
6. Jābir ؓ continued and said, "We did not have any other intention but that of *Ḥajj* only, being unaware of the *ʿUmrah* (at that season).
7. When we came with him to the *Kaʿbah*, he ﷺ touched the black stone.
8. Then he ﷺ made seven circuits around the *Kaʿbah.*
9. He ﷺ ran three of them and walked the remaining four.
10. And then going to the Station of Ibrāhīm, he ﷺ recited, "*And adopt the Station of Ibrāhīm as a place of prayer.*" (2:125)
11. He ﷺ then prayed two units of prayer with the station between him and the *Kaʿbah.*
12. In one narration it states he ﷺ recited, "Say, He is Allāh, The One" and "Say, O unbelievers."
13. He ﷺ then returned to the black stone and kissed it.
14. He ﷺ then went out of the gate to Al Ṣafā.

٤. أَهَلَّ النَّاسُ بِهَذَا الذِي يُهِلُّونَ بِهِ، فَلَمْ يَرُدَّ رَسُولُ اللَّهِ ﷺ عَلَيْهِمْ شَيْئًا مِنْهُ،

٥. وَلَزِمَ رَسُولُ اللَّهِ ﷺ تَلْبِيَتَهُ.

٦. قَالَ جَابِرٌ: لَسْنَا نَنْوِي إِلَّا الحَجَّ، لَسْنَا نَعْرِفُ العُمْرَةَ.

٧. حَتَّى إِذَا أَتَيْنَا البَيْتَ مَعَهُ اِسْتَلَمَ الرُّكْنَ،

٨. فَطَافَ سَبْعًا

٩. فَرَمَلَ ثَلَاثًا وَمَشَى أَرْبَعًا،

١٠. ثُمَّ نَفَذَ إِلَى مَقَامِ إِبْرَاهِيمَ فَقَرَأَ: ﴿وَٱتَّخِذُوا۟ مِن مَّقَامِ إِبْرَٰهِـۧمَ مُصَلًّى﴾ [البَقَرَة: ١٢٥]

١١. فَصَلَّى رَكْعَتَيْنِ، فَجَعَلَ المَقَامَ بَيْنَهُ وَبَيْنَ البَيْتِ.

١٢. وَفِي رِوَايَةٍ: «أَنَّهُ قَرَأَ فِي الرَّكْعَتَيْنِ: «قُلْ هُوَ اللَّهُ أَحَدٌ.» وَ «قُلْ يَا أَيُّهَا الكَافِرُونَ.»

١٣. ثُمَّ رَجَعَ إِلَى الرُّكْنِ وَاسْتَلَمَهُ،

١٤. ثُمَّ خَرَجَ مِنْ البَابِ إِلَى الصَّفَا،

15. And as he ﷺ reached near it, he recited, "*Verily Al-Ṣafā and al-Marwāh are among the signs appointed by Allāh.*" (2:158).
16. He ﷺ first mounted al-Ṣafā till he saw the House.
17. Then he ﷺ faced the *Qiblah.*
18. He ﷺ then declared the Oneness of Allāh ﷻ, glorified Him and said,

لا إِلَهَ إلا اللَّهُ وَحْدَهُ لا شَرِيكَ لَهُ، لَهُ الْمُلْكُ، وَلَهُ الحَمْدُ، وَهُوَ عَلَى كُلِّ شَيْءٍ قَدِيرٌ، لا إِلَهَ إلا اللَّهُ وَحده أَنْجَزَ وَعْدَهُ، وَنَصرَ عَبْدَهُ، وَهَزَمَ الأَحْزَابَ وَحْدَهُ

"*Lā ilāha illal-lāh waḥdahu lā sharīka lah, lahul-mulk walahul ḥamd wa huwa ʿalā kulli shayʾin qadīr, lā ilāha illala-lāh waḥdah, anjaza waʿdah, wa naṣara ʿabdah, wa hazamal-aḥzāba waḥdah.*"

"There is no god but Allāh, One, there is no partner with Him. His is the Sovereignty, to Him praise is due and He is Powerful over everything. There is no god but Allāh alone, Who fulfilled His promise, helped His servant and routed the confederates alone." He said these words three times making supplications in between.

19. He ﷺ then descended and walked towards *al-Marwah*
20. And when his ﷺ feet touched the bottom of the valley, he ﷺ ran.
21. And when he ﷺ began to ascend, he ﷺ walked.

١٥. فَلَمَّا دنَا مِنْ الصَّفَا قَرَأَ: ﴿إِنَّ ٱلصَّفَا وَٱلْمَرْوَةَ مِن شَعَآئِرِ ٱللَّهِۖ﴾ [البَقَرَة: ١٥٨].

١٦. فَرَقَى عَلَيْهِ حَتَّى رَأَى البَيْتَ،

١٧. فَاسْتَقْبَلَ القِبْلَةَ،

١٨. فَوَحَّدَ اللهَ وَكَبَّرَهُ، وَقَالَ: «لَا إِلَهَ إِلَّا اللَّهُ وَحْدَهُ لَا شَرِيكَ لَهُ، لَهُ المُلْكُ وَلَهُ الحَمْدُ، وَهُوَ عَلَى كُلِّ شَيْءٍ قَدِيرٌ، لَا إِلَهَ إِلَّا اللَّهُ وَحْدَهُ، أَنْجَزَ وَعْدَهُ، وَنَصَرَ عَبْدَهُ، وَهَزَمَ الأَحْزَابَ وَحْدَهُ.» ثُمَّ دَعَا بَيْنَ ذَلِكَ، قَالَ مِثْلَ هَذَا ثَلَاثَ مَرَّاتٍ.

١٩. ثُمَّ نَزَلَ وَمَشَى إِلَى الْمَرْوَة،

٢٠. حَتَّى إِذَا انْصَبَّتْ قَدَمَاهُ فِي بَطْنِ الوَادِي سَعَى،

٢١. حَتَّى إِذَا صَعَدَتَا مَشَى،

22. Until he ﷺ reached *al-Marwah.* There, he did as he ﷺ had done at *al-Ṣafā.*
23. When it was his last running at *al-Marwah* he ﷺ said, "If I had known beforehand what I have come to know afterwards, I would not have brought sacrificial animals and would have performed an *ʿUmrah.* So, whoever among you does not have the sacrificial animals with him should leave the *Iḥrām* and treat it as an *ʿUmrah.*
24. Surāqah ibn Mālik ibn Juʿsham ؓ got up and said, "O Messenger of Allāh ﷺ, does it apply to the present year, or does it apply forever?" Thereupon the Messenger of Allāh ﷺ intertwined his fingers and said twice, "The *ʿUmrah* has become incorporated in the *Ḥajj*" adding, "No, but forever and ever."
25. ʿAli ؓ came from the Yemen with the sacrificial animals for the Prophet ﷺ and found Fāṭimah ؓ to be one among those who left the state of *Iḥrām* and had put on dyed clothes and had applied *koḥl.* ʿAli ؓ disapproved of what she had done, whereupon she said, "My father has commanded me to do this." He (the narrator) said that ʿAli ؓ used to say in ʿIrāq, "I went to the Messenger of Allāh ﷺ showing annoyance at Fāṭimah ؓ for what she had done, and asked the (verdict) of Allāh's Messenger ﷺ regarding what she had narrated from him, and told him that I was angry with her, whereupon he said, "She has told the truth, she has told the truth."

٢٢. حَتَّى أَتَى المرْوَةَ فَفَعَلَ عَلَى المرْوَةِ كَمَا فَعَلَ عَلَى الصَّفَا،

٢٣. حَتَّى إِذَا كَانَ آخِرُ طَوَافِهِ عَلَى المرْوَةِ، فَقَالَ: «لَوْ أَنِّي اِسْتَقْبَلْتُ مِنْ أَمْرِي مَا اِسْتَدْبَرْتُ لَمْ أَسُقْ الهَدْيَ، وَجَعَلْتُهَا عُمْرَةً، فَمَنْ كَانَ مِنْكُمْ لَيْسَ مَعَهُ هَدْيٌ فَلْيُحِلَّ وَلْيَجْعَلْهَا عُمْرَةً.»

٢٤. فَقَامَ سُرَاقَةُ بْنُ مَالِكِ بْنِ جُعْشُمٍ، فَقَالَ: يَا رَسُولَ اللَّهِ، أَلِعَامِنَا هَذَا، أَمْ لِأَبَدٍ؟ فَشَبَّكَ رَسُولُ اللَّهِ ﷺ أَصَابِعَهُ وَاحِدَةً فِي الأُخْرَى، وَقَالَ: دَخَلَتْ العُمْرَةُ فِي الحَجِّ مَرَّتَيْنِ لَا، بَلْ لِأَبَدِ أَبَدٍ.

٢٥. وَقَدِمَ عَلِيٌّ مِنْ اليَمَنِ بِبُدْنِ النَّبِيِّ ﷺ فَوَجَدَ فَاطِمَةَ مِمَّنْ حَلَّ، وَلَبِسَتْ ثِيَابًا صَبِيغًا وَاكْتَحَلَتْ، فَأَنْكَرَ ذَلِكَ عَلَيْهَا، فَقَالَتْ: إِنَّ أَبِي أَمَرَنِي بِهَذَا، قَالَ: فَكَانَ عَلِيٌّ يَقُولُ، بِالعِرَاقِ: فَذَهَبْتُ إِلَى رَسُولِ اللَّهِ ﷺ مُحَرِّشًا عَلَى فَاطِمَةَ لِلَّذِي صَنَعَتْ، مُسْتَفْتِيًا لِرَسُولِ اللَّهِ ﷺ فِيمَا ذَكَرَتْ عَنْهُ، فَأَخْبَرْتُهُ أَنِّي أَنْكَرْتُ ذَلِكَ عَلَيْهَا، فَقَالَ صَدَقَتْ صَدَقَتْ

(The Prophet ﷺ then asked ʿAli) "What did you say when you undertook to go for *Ḥajj*? I (ʿAli) said, "O Allāh, I am entering the state of *Iḥrām* for the same purpose as the Messenger has put it on." He ﷺ said, "I have with me sacrificial animals, so do not leave the state of *Iḥrām*."

26. He (Jābir ﵁) said, "The total number of those sacrificial animals brought by ʿAli ﵁ from the Yemen and of those brought by the Messenger ﷺ was one hundred.
27. Then all the people, except the Messenger ﷺ and those who had with them sacrificial animals, left the state of *Iḥrām*, and got their hair clipped.
28. When it was the day of *Tarwiyah* (8th of Dhul-Ḥijjah) they all went to Minā.
29. Then they entered the state of *Iḥrām* for *Ḥajj*.
30. The Messenger of Allāh ﷺ rode and led the *Ẓuhr*, *ʿAṣr*, *Maghrib*, *ʿIshāʾ* and *Fajr* prayers.
31. He ﷺ then waited a little till the sun rose.
32. And commanded that a tent of hair should be pitched at Namirah. The Messenger of Allāh ﷺ then set out and the Quraish did not doubt that he would halt at *al-Mashʿar al-Ḥarām* (the sacred site) as the Quraish used to do in the pre-Islamic period. The Messenger of Allāh ﷺ, however, passed until he ﷺ came to ʿArafah and he ﷺ found that the tent had been pitched for him ﷺ at Namirah.

مَاذَا قُلْتَ حِينَ فَرَضْتَ الحَجَّ؟» قَالَ: قُلْتُ: «اللَّهُمَّ إِنِّي أُهِلُّ بِمَا أَهَلَّ بِهِ رَسُولُكَ. قَالَ: فَإِنَّ مَعِيَ الهَدْيَ فَلَا تَحِلَّ.»

٢٦. قَالَ: فَكَانَ جَمَاعَةُ الهَدْيِ الذِي قَدِمَ بِهِ عَلِيٌّ مِنْ اليَمَنِ، وَالذِي أَتَى بِهِ النَّبِيُّ ﷺ مِائَةً.

٢٧. قَالَ: فَحَلَّ النَّاسُ كُلُّهُمْ، وَقَصَّرُوا، إِلَّا النَّبِيَّ ﷺ وَمَنْ كَانَ مَعَهُ هَدْيٌ.

٢٨. فَلَمَّا كَانَ يَوْمُ التَّرْوِيَةِ تَوَجَّهُوا إِلَى مِنًى.

٢٩. فَأَهَلُّوا بِالْحَجِّ.

٣٠. وَرَكِبَ النَّبِيُّ ﷺ فَصَلَّى بِهَا الظُّهْرَ وَالْعَصْرَ، وَالْمَغْرِبَ وَالْعِشَاءَ وَالْفَجْرَ،

٣١. ثُمَّ مَكَثَ قَلِيلًا حَتَّى طَلَعَتْ الشَّمْسُ،

٣٢.وَأَمَرَ بِقُبَّةٍ مَنْ شَعَرٍ تُضْرَبُ لَهُ بِنَمِرَةَ فَسَارَ رَسُولُ اللَّهِ ﷺ ، وَلَا تَشُكُّ قُرَيْشٌ إِلَّا أَنَّهُ وَاقِفٌ عِنْدَ المشْعَرِ الحَرَامِ، كَمَا كَانَتْ قُرَيْشٌ تَصْنَعُ فِي الجَاهِلِيَّةِ. فَأَجَازَ رَسُولُ اللَّهِ ﷺ، حَتَّى أَتَى عَرَفَةَ، فَوَجَدَ القُبَّةَ قَدْ ضُرِبَتْ لَهُ بِنَمِرَةَ، فَنَزَلَ بِهَا

33. There he ﷺ got down till the sun had passed the meridian; he ﷺ commanded that al-Qaṣwāʾ should be brought and saddled for him ﷺ.

34. Then he ﷺ came to the bottom of the valley and addressed the people saying, "Verily your blood, your properties are as sacred and inviolable as the sacredness of this day of yours, in this month of yours, in this town of yours. Behold! Everything pertaining to the Days of Ignorance is under my feet, completely abolished. Abolished are also the blood-revenges of the Days of Ignorance. The first claim of ours on blood-revenge which I abolish is that of the son of Rabīʿah ibn al-Ḥārith, who was nursed among the tribe of Saʿd and killed by Hudhail. Moreover, the usury of the pre-Islamic period is abolished, and the first of our usury I abolish is that of ʿAbbās ibn ʿAbd al-Muṭṭalib, for it is all abolished. Fear Allāh concerning women! Verily you have taken them on the security of Allāh, and intercourse with them has been made lawful unto you by words of Allāh. You too have right over them, and that they should not allow anyone to sit on your bed that you do not like. But if they do that, you can chastise them but not severely. Their rights upon you are that you should provide them with food and clothing in a fitting manner. I have left among you the Book of Allāh, and if you hold fast to it, you would never go astray.

٣٣. حَتَّى إِذَا زَاغَتْ الشَّمْسُ أَمَرَ بِالْقَصْوَاءِ فَرُحِلَتْ لَهُ،

٣٤. فَأَتَى بَطْنَ الوَادِي فَخَطَبَ النَّاسَ: وَقَالَ: «إِنَّ دِمَاءَكُمْ وَأَمْوَالَكُمْ حَرَامٌ عَلَيْكُمْ، كَحُرْمَةِ يَوْمِكُمْ هَذَا، فِي شَهْرِكُمْ هَذَا، فِي بَلَدِكُمْ هَذَا، أَلَا كُلُّ شَيْءٍ مِنْ أَمْرِ الجَاهِلِيَّةِ تَحْتَ قَدَمَيَّ مَوْضُوعٌ، وَدِمَاءُ الجَاهِلِيَّةِ مَوْضُوعَةٌ، وَإِنَّ أَوَّلَ دَمٍ أَضَعُ مِنْ دِمَائِنَا: دَمُ اِبْنِ رَبِيعَةَ بْنِ الحَارِثِ – كَانَ مُسْتَرْضِعًا فِي بَنِي سَعْدٍ فَقَتَلَتْهُ هُذَيْلٌ –، وَرِبَا الجَاهِلِيَّةِ مَوْضُوعٌ، وَأَوَّلُ رِبًا أَضَعُ مِنْ رِبَانَا رِبَا عَبَّاسِ بْنَ عَبْدِ المطَّلِبِ، فَإِنَّهُ مَوْضُوعٌ كُلُّهُ، فَاتَّقُوا اللَّهَ فِي النِّسَاءِ، فَإِنَّكُمْ أَخَذْتُمُوهُنَّ بِأَمَانَةِ اللَّهِ، وَاسْتَحْلَلْتُمْ فُرُوجَهُنَّ بِكَلِمَةِ اللَّهِ، وَلَكُمْ عَلَيْهِنَّ أَنْ لَا يُوطِئْنَ فُرُشَكُمْ أَحَدًا تَكْرَهُونَهُ، فَإِنْ فَعَلْنَ ذَلِكَ فَاضْرِبُوهُنَّ ضَرْبًا غَيْرَ مُبَرِّحٍ، وَلَهُنَّ عَلَيْكُمْ رِزْقُهُنَّ وَكِسْوَتُهُنَّ بِالْمَعْرُوفِ. وَقَدْ تَرَكْتُ فِيكُمْ مَا لَنْ تَضِلُّوا بَعْدَهُ إِنْ اِعْتَصَمْتُمْ بِهِ: كِتَابُ اللَّهِ.

You will all be asked about me (on the Day of Resurrection), (now tell me) what would you say? They (the audience) said, "We will bear witness that you have conveyed (the message), discharged (the ministry of Prophethood) and given wise (sincere) counsel." He (the narrator) said, "He ﷺ then raised his forefinger towards the sky and pointing it at the people (said), "O Allāh, be witness. O Allāh, be witness," saying it thrice.

35. (Bilāl ﷺ then) pronounced Adhān and later on Iqāmah and he ﷺ led the *Ẓuhr* prayer. He (Bilāl ﷺ) then uttered Iqāmah and he ﷺ led the *ʿAṣr* prayer.
36. And he ﷺ observed no other prayer in between the two.
37. The Messenger of Allāh ﷺ then mounted his camel and came to the place of stay.
38. He ﷺ made his she-camel al-Qaṣwāʾ, turn towards the side where there are rocks, having the path taken by those who went on foot in front of him, and faced the Qiblah.
39. He ﷺ kept standing there till the sun set, and the yellow light had somewhat gone, and the disc of the sun had disappeared.
40. He ﷺ made Usāmah ﷺ sit behind him and he pulled the nose-string of al-Qaṣwāʾ so forcefully that its head touched the saddle (in order to keep her under perfect control).

وَأَنْتُمْ تُسْالون عَنِّي، فَمَا أَنْتُمْ قَائِلُونَ؟ قَالُوا: نَشْهَدُ أَنَّكَ قَدْ بَلَّغْتَ، وَأَدَّيْتَ، وَنَصَحْتَ، فَقَالَ بِإِصْبُعِهِ السَّبَّابَةِ يَرْفَعُهَا إِلَى السَّمَاءِ وَيَنْكُبُهَا إِلَى النَّاسِ: اللَّهُمَّ اِشْهَدْ، اللَّهُمَّ اِشْهَدْ، ثَلَاثَ مَرَّاتٍ.

٣٥. ثُمَّ أَذَّنَ بِلَالٌ، ثُمَّ أَقَامَ فَصَلَّى الظُّهْرَ، ثُمَّ أَقَامَ فَصَلَّى العَصْرَ،

٣٦. وَلَمْ يُصَلِّ بَيْنَهُمَا شَيْئًا.

٣٧. ثُمَّ رَكِبَ حَتَّى أَتَى المَوْقِفَ،

٣٨. فَجَعَلَ بَطْنَ نَاقَتِهِ القَصْوَاءِ إِلَى الصَّخَرَاتِ وَجَعَلَ حَبْلَ المشَاةِ بَيْنَ يَدَيْهِ، وَاسْتَقْبَلَ القِبْلَةَ،

٣٩. فَلَمْ يَزَلْ وَاقِفًا حَتَّى غَرَبَتْ الشَّمْسُ، وَذَهَبَتْ الصَّفْرَةُ قَلِيلًا حَتَّى غَابَ القُرْصُ،

٤٠. وَأَرْدَفَ أُسَامَةُ بنْ زَيْدٍ خَلْفَهُ، وَدَفَعَ رَسُولُ اللهِ صَلَّى اللهُ عَلَيْهِ وَسَلَّمَ، وَقَدْ شَنَقَ لِلْقَصْوَاءِ الزِّمَامَ حَتَّى إِنَّ رَأْسَهَا لَيُصِيبُ مَوْرِكَ رَحْلِهِ.

41. He ﷺ then pointed out to the people with his right hand to be moderate (in speed), and whenever he happened to pass over an elevated tract of sand, he ﷺ slightly loosened it (the nose-string of his camel) till she climbed up.
42. This is how he ﷺ reached al-Muzdalifah.
43. There he ﷺ led the *Maghrib* and *ʿIshāʾ* prayers with one *Adhān* and two *Iqāmahs*
44. and did not glorify (Allāh ﷻ) in between them.
45. The Messenger of Allāh ﷺ then lay down till dawn.
46. He ﷺ offered the *Fajr* prayer with an *Adhān* and *Iqāmah* when the morning light was clear.
47. He ﷺ again mounted al-Qaṣwāʾ, and when he ﷺ came *to al-Mashʿar al-Ḥarām*,
48. he ﷺ faced the *Qiblah*,
49. supplicated to Him ﷻ, Glorified Him ﷻ, and pronounced His ﷻ Uniqueness and Oneness,
50. and kept standing till the daylight was very clear.
51. He ﷺ then went quickly before the sun rose,
52. and seated behind him was al-Faḍl ibn al ʿAbbās رضي الله عنه ... till he came to the bottom of Muḥassar. He ﷺ urged her (al-Qaṣwāʾ) a little,

٤١. وَيقُولُ بِيَدِهِ اليُمْنَى: «أَيُّهَا النَّاسُ، السَّكِينَةَ، السَّكِينَةَ» كُلَّمَا أَتَى حَبْلًا مِنْ الحِبَالِ أَرْخَى لَهَا قَلِيلًا حَتَّى تصْعَدَ،

٤٢. حَتَّى أَتَى المزْدَلِفَةَ،

٤٣. فَصَلَّى بِهَا المغْرِبَ وَالْعِشَاءَ بِأَذَانٍ وَاحِدٍ وَإِقَامَتَيْنِ،

٤٤. وَلَمْ يُسَبِّحْ بَيْنَهُمَا شَيْئًا،

٤٥. ثُمَّ اِضْطَجَعَ حَتَّى طَلَعَ الفَجْرُ

٤٦. وصَلَّى الفَجْرَ حِينَ تَبَيَّنَ لَهُ الصُّبْحُ بِأَذَانٍ وَإِقَامَةٍ،

٤٧. ثُم رَكِبَ القَصْوَاءَ حَتَّى أَتَى الْمَشْعَرَ الحَرَامَ،

٤٨. فَاسْتَقْبَلَ القِبْلَةَ،

٤٩. فَدَعَاهُ، وَكَبَّرَهُ، وهَلَّلَهُ، وَوَحَّدَهُ

٥٠. فَلَمْ يَزَلْ وَاقِفًا حَتَّى أَسْفَرَ جِدًّا،

٥١. فَدَفَعَ قَبْلَ أَنْ تَطْلُعَ الشَّمْسُ

٥٢. وَأَرْدَفَ الفَضْلَ بْنَ العَبَّاسِ.... حَتَّى أَتَى بَطْنَ مُحَسِّرٍ فَحَرَّكَ قَلِيلًا،

53. and following the middle road, which comes out at the greatest *jamrah*
54. he ﷺ came to the *jamrah* which is near the tree and then threw seven small pebbles at it
55. saying *Allāhu Akbar* while throwing each one of them
56. in a manner in which the small pebbles are thrown (with the help of fingers)
57. and he ﷺ did this in the bottom of the valley.
58. He ﷺ then went to the place of sacrifice,
59. and sacrificed sixty-three (camels) with his own hand.
60. Then he ﷺ gave the remaining number to ʿAli ﷺ who sacrificed them and shared with him in his sacrifice.
61. He ﷺ then commanded that a piece of flesh from each animal sacrificed should be put in a pot, and when it was cooked, both of them (the Prophet and ʿAli) took some meat out of it and drank its soup.
62. The Messenger of Allāh ﷺ again rode and came to the *Kaʿbah*,
63. and offered the *Ẓuhr* prayer at Makkah.
64. He ﷺ came to the tribe of ʿAbd al-Muṭṭalib, who were supplying water at Zamzam and said, "Draw water O tribe of ʿAbd al-Muttalib; were it not that people would usurp this right of supplying water from you, I would have drawn it along with you. So, they handed him a bucket and he drank from it." (reported by Muslim).

٥٣. ثُمَّ سَلَكَ الطَّرِيقَ الوُسْطَى الَّتِي تَخْرُجُ عَلَى الجَمْرَةِ الكُبْرَى،

٥٤. حَتَّى أَتَى الجَمْرَةَ الَّتِي عِنْدَ الشَّجَرَةِ فَرَمَاهَا بِسَبْعِ حَصَيَاتٍ

٥٥. يُكَبِّرُ مَعَ كُلِّ حَصَاةٍ مِنْهَا

٥٦. مِثْل حَصَى الخَذْف

٥٧. رَمَى مِنْ بَطْنِ الوَادِي،

٥٨. ثُم انْصَرَفَ إِلى الْمَنْحَرِ،

٥٩. فَنَحَرَ ثَلاثًا وَسِتِّينَ بِيَدِهِ،

٦٠. ثُمَّ أَعْطَى عَلِيًّا فَنَحَرَ مَا غَبَرَ، وَأَشْرَكَهُ فِي هَدْيِهِ،

٦١. ثُمَّ أَمَرَ مِنْ كُلِّ بُدْنَةٍ بِبِضْعة، فَجُعِلَتْ فِي قِدْرٍ، وطُبِخَتْ، فَأَكَلا مِنْ لَحْمِهَا، وَشَرَبَا مِنْ مَرَقِهَا

٦٢. ثُمَّ رَكِبَ رَسُولُ اللهِ صَلَّى اللهُ عَلَيْهِ وسَلَّم فَأَفَاضَ إِلَى البَيْتِ

٦٣. فَصَلَّى بِمَكَّةَ الظُّهْرَ،

٦٤. فَأَتَى بَنِي عَبْدِ المطَّلِبِ، يَسْقُونَ عَلَى زَمْزَمَ، فَقَالَ: «انْزِعُوا بَنِي عَبْدِ المطَّلِبِ، فَلَوْلَا أَنْ يَغْلِبَكُمُ النَّاسُ عَلَى سِقَايَتِكُمْ لَنَزَعْتُ مَعَكُمْ، فَنَاوَلُوهُ دَلْوًا فَشَرِبَ مِنْهُ.» رَوَاهُ مُسْلِمٌ

273. When the Prophet ﷺ would perform the rites he would say, "Take from me your rites." Thus, the most complete pilgrimage is by following the example of the Prophet ﷺ and his companions.

274. If a pilgrim restricted himself to the following, it will suffice him:

a. The four pillars (*arkān*):
   1. *Iḥrām*
   2. The standing at *ʿArafah*
   3. The *Ṭawāf*
   4. The running between *al-Ṣafā & al-Marwah*

b. As well as the obligations:
   1. To be in the state of *iḥrām* from the designated point (*mīqāt)*
   2. To stay in ʿArafah until sunset
   3. To stay overnight in Muzdalifah the night before the sacrifice
   4. And to spend the days of *Tashrīq* in Mina
   5. To throw the stones at the *Jamarāt*
   6. To shave or shorten one's hair

٢٧٣. وَكَانَ ﷺ يَفْعَلُ المنَاسِكَ، وَيَقُولُ لِلنَّاسِ: «خُذُوا عَنِّي مَنَاسِكَكُمْ.» فَأَكْمَلُ مَا يَكُونُ مِنَ الحَجِّ: الاقْتِدَاءُ بِالنَّبِيِّ ﷺ فِيهِ وَأَصْحَابِهِ رَضِيَ اللَّهُ عَنْهُمْ.

٢٧٤. وَلَوْ اِقْتَصَرَ الحَاجُّ عَلَى:

أ- الأَرْكَانِ الأَرْبَعَةِ التِي هِيَ:

١. الإِحْرَامُ،

٢. وَالْوُقُوفُ بِعَرَفَةَ،

٣. وَالطَّوَافُ،

٤. وَالسَّعْيُ.

ب- وَالْوَاجِبَاتِ التِي هِيَ:

١. الإِحْرَامُ مِنْ الميقَاتِ،

٢. وَالْوُقُوفُ بِعَرَفَةَ إِلَى الغُرُوبِ،

٣. وَالْمَبِيتُ لَيْلَةَ النَّحْرِ بِمُزْدَلِفَة

٤. وَلَيَالِي أَيَّامِ التَّشْرِيقِ بِمِنًى،

٥. وَرَمْيُ الجِمَارِ،

٦. وَالحَلْقُ أَوْ التَّقْصِيرُ لَأَجْزَأَهُ ذَلِكَ.

275. The difference between leaving out a pillar (*rukn*) in Ḥajj and leaving out an obligation (*wājib*) is as follows:

- The one who leaves out a pillar will not have their Ḥajj accepted until one performs the pillar in the prescribed manner.
- As for the one who leaves out an obligation, their Ḥajj will be acceptable and correct, however, they will be sinful and must offer a sacrifice due to leaving out the obligation.

276. A person who wishes to enter the state of *iḥrām* is given the choice of performing the *tamattuᶜ* method of Ḥajj – which is the best – or *Qirān* or *Ifrād.*

277. *Tamattuᶜ* is done by: entering the state of *iḥrām* and intending to do *ᶜUmrah* in the months of Ḥajj, then completing the *ᶜUmrah* and then leaving the state of *iḥrām*, then re-entering it for Ḥajj in the same year.

278. *Ifrād* is done by: entering the state of *iḥrām* for Ḥajj only.

279. *Qirān* is done by: entering the state of *iḥrām* to perform both (i.e. *ᶜUmrah* & *Ḥajj*) or to enter *iḥrām* for *ᶜUmrah* then include the *Ḥajj* to be a part of it before one begins doing the *ṭawāf.*

٢٧٥. وَالْفَرْقُ بَيْنَ تَرْكِ الرُّكْنِ فِي الحَجِّ وَتَرْكِ الوَاجِبِ:

- أَنَّ تَارِكَ الرُّكْنِ لا يَصِحُّ حَجُّهُ حَتَّى يَفْعَلَهُ عَلَى صِفَتِهِ الشَّرْعِيَّةِ

- وَتَارِكَ الوَاجِبِ، حَجُّهُ صَحِيحٌ، وَعَلَيْهِ إِثْمٌ وَدَمٌ لِتَرْكِهِ

٢٧٦. وَيُخَيَّرُ مَنْ يُرِيدُ الإِحْرَامَ بَيْنَ التَّمَتُّعِ -وَهُوَ أَفْضَلُ- وَالْقِرَانِ وَالإِفْرَادِ.

٢٧٧. فَالتَّمَتُّعُ هُوَ: أَنْ يُحْرِمَ بِالْعُمْرَةِ فِي أَشْهُرِ الْحَجِّ، وَيَفْرُغُ مِنْهَا، ثُمَّ يُحْرِمَ بِالْحَجِّ مِنْ عَامِهِ،

- وَعَلَيْهِ دَمٌ إِنْ لَمْ يَكُنْ مِنْ حَاضِرِي المسْجِدِ الحَرَامِ.

٢٧٨. وَالإِفْرَادُ هُوَ: أَنْ يُحْرِمَ بِالْحَجِّ مُفْرِدًا.

٢٧٩. وَالْقِرَانُ:

أَ- أَنْ يُحْرِمَ بِهِمَا مَعًا.

بِ- أَوْ يُحْرِمُ بِالْعُمْرَةِ، ثُمَّ يُدْخِلُ الحَجَّ عَلَيْهَا قَبْلَ الشُّرُوعِ فِي طَوَافِهَا.

280. The one who opts for *tamattuʿ* is required to adopt the method (of *qirān*):

1. If one was worried that they would miss the standing at *ʿArafah* due to being preoccupied by performing an *ʿŪmrah.*
2. If a woman menstruated or had post-natal bleeding, whilst knowing she would not become pure prior to the time of the standing at *ʿArafah.*

281. The actions of the *mufrid* and the *qārin* are the same. However, the *qārin* must offer a sacrifice whereas the *mufrid* does not.

282. The *muḥrim* must avoid the following matters when entering into the inviolable state:

1. Cutting hair
2. Clipping nails
3. To wear tailored clothing (applicable to men)
4. Covering the head (applicable to men)
5. Perfuming oneself, this applies to men and women.
6. Likewise, it is prohibited upon the *muḥrim* to kill game, or to direct one towards it or to assist another in it.
7. The most important matter to avoid whilst in a state of *iḥrām* is sexual intercourse. This is because it has

٢٨٠. وَيُضْطَرُّ المتَمَتِّعُ إِلَى هَذِهِ الصِّفَةِ:

١- إِذَا خَافَ فَوَاتَ الوُقُوفِ بِعَرَفَةَ إِذَا اشْتَغَلَ بِعُمْرَتِهِ

٢- وَإِذَا حَاضَتْ الْمَرْأَةُ أَوْ نَفِسَتْ، وَعَرَفَتْ أَنَّهَا لا تَطْهُرُ قَبْلَ وَقْتِ الوُقُوفِ بِعَرَفَةَ.

٢٨١. والْمُفْرِدُ والقَارِنُ فِعْلُهُمَا وَاحِدٌ، وَعَلَى القَارِنِ هَدْيٌ دُوْنَ الْمُفْرِدِ.

٢٨٢. وَيَجْتَنِبُ المحْرِمُ وَقْتَ إِحْرَامِهِ:

١. حَلْقَ الشَّعْرِ،

٢. وَتَقْلِيمَ الأَظْفَارِ،

٣. وَلُبْسَ المخِيطِ، إِنْ كَانَ رَجُلاً

٤. وَتَغْطِيَةَ رَأْسِهِ إِنْ كَانَ رَجُلاً،

٥. وَالطِّيبَ رَجُلاً وَامْرَأَةً،

٦.وَكَذَا يَحْرُمُ عَلَى المحْرِمِ: قَتْلُ صَيْدِ البَرِّ الوَحْشِيِّ المأْكُولِ، وَالدَّلالَةُ عَلَيْهِ، وَالْإِعَانَةُ عَلَى قَتْلِهِ.

٧. وَأَعْظَمُ مَحْظُورَاتِ الإِحْرَامِ: الجِمَاعُ:

been emphatically prohibited and it nullifies one's rites and obligates atonement by offering a camel.

283. *Fidyah al adhā* (expiation for violating the *iḥrām*):

If a man covers his head, or wears tailored clothing, or if a woman covers her face or wears gloves or uses perfume, they will be given the choice of doing the following:

1. Fast three days
2. Feed six poor people
3. Slaughter a sheep

284. If a person kills game then they are given the following options:

1. To offer in sacrifice an animal similar to the one killed.
2. To estimate the value of the killed game and buy food with that amount to feed the poor, giving each person a handful of wheat or half a *ṣāᶜ* of something else.
3. If one is unable to feed the poor, they should fast a day for each poor person they were meant to feed.

285. The sacrificial animals offered for *tamattuᶜ* & *qirān* must fulfil the conditions for the animal offered for *uḍḥīyah.*

لِأَنَّهُ مُغَلَّظٌ تَحْرِيمُهُ مُفْسِدٌ لِلنُّسُكِ، مُوجِبٌ لِفِدْيَةٍ بَدَنَةٍ.

٢٨٣. وَأَمَّا فِدْيَةُ الأَذَى:

إِذَا غَطَّى رَأْسَهُ، أَوْ لَبِسَ المخِيطَ، أَوْ غطَّتْ المرْأَةُ وَجْهَهَا، أَوْ لَبِسَتِ القُفَّازَيْنِ، أَوْ اِسْتَعْمَلَا الطِّيبَ، فَيُخَيَّرُ بَيْنَ:

١. صِيَامِ ثَلَاثَةِ أَيَّامٍ،

٢. أَوْ إِطْعَامِ سِتَّةِ مَسَاكِينَ،

٣. أَوْ ذَبْحِ شَاةٍ.

٢٨٤. وَإِذَا قَتَلَ الصَّيْدَ خُيِّرَ بَيْنَ:

١. ذَبْحِ مِثْلِهِ - إِنْ كَانَ لَهُ مِثْلٌ مِنَ النَّعَمِ.

٢. وَبَيْنَ تَقْوِيمِ المِثْلِ بِمَحَلِّ الإِتْلَافِ، فَيَشْتَرِي بِهِ طَعَامًا فَيُطْعِمَهُ، لِكُلِّ مِسْكِينٍ مُدُّ بُرٍّ، أَوْ نِصْفُ صَاعٍ مِنْ غَيْرِهِ،

٣. أَوْ يَصُومُ عَنْ إِطْعَامِ كُلِّ مِسْكِينٍ يَوْمًا.

٢٨٥. وَأَمَّا دَمُ المتْعَةِ وَالْقِرَانِ فَيَجِبُ فِيهِمَا مَا يُجْزِئُ فِي الأُضْحِيَّةِ.

286. However, if one was unable to find a sacrificial animal, then they should fast ten days; three in Ḥajj - it is permissible to do these fasts in the days of *tashrīq* - and the remaining seven should be done when one returns home.

287. The same ruling is given if:

1. A person leaves out an obligation.
2. If a person is required to pay the *fidyah* due to intercourse.

288. Every sacrifice or food that is given as expiation and is associated with the sacred precinct (*ḥaram*) or the *iḥrām,* is to be given to the poor of the *ḥaram* whether they were residents or visitors of the *ḥaram.*

289. Fasting can be done anywhere.

290. It is recommended to eat from the sacrificial offering for rites such as for *tamattuʿ*, *qirān* and *hadiy,* as well as to give some away as a gift and as charity.

291. It is not permitted to eat from the obligatory sacrificial offering resulting from committing a *maḥẓūr* (prohibited act in the state of *iḥrām*) or leaving out an obligation. Such an offering is called *dạm jubrān.* Instead, one has to give all of it away as charity since it is treated as an expiation (*kaffārah*).

٢٨٦. فَإِنْ لَمْ يَجِدْ صَامَ عَشَرَةَ أَيَّامٍ: ثَلَاثَةً فِي الحَجِّ، وَيَجُوزُ أَنْ يَصُومَ أَيَّامَ التَّشْرِيقِ عَنْهَا وَسَبْعَةً إِذَا رَجَعَ.

٢٨٧. وَكَذَلِكَ حُكْمُ:

١. مَنْ تَرَكَ وَاجِبًا،

٢. أَوْ وَجَبَتْ عَلَيْهِ الفِدْيَةُ لِمُبَاشَرَةٍ.

٢٨٨. وَكُلُّ هَدْيٍ أَوْ إِطْعَامٍ يَتَعَلَّقُ بِحَرَمٍ أَوْ إِحْرَامٍ: فَلِمَسَاكِينِ الحَرَمِ مِنْ مُقِيمٍ وَأُفُقِيٍّ.

٢٨٩. وَيُجْزِئُ الصَّوْمُ بِكُلِّ مَكَانٍ.

٢٩٠. وَدَمُ النُّسُكِ كَالْمُتْعَةِ وَالْقِرَانِ وَالْهَدْيِ، المسْتَحَبُّ: أَنْ يَأْكُلَ مِنْهُ وَيُهْدِي وَيَتَصَدَّقَ.

٢٩١. وَالدَّمُ الوَاجِبُ لِفِعْلِ المحْظُورِ، أَوْ تَرْكِ الوَاجِبِ – وَيُسَمَّى دَمَ جُبْرَانٍ– لَا يَأْكُلُ مِنْهُ شَيْئًا، بَلْ يَتَصَدَّقُ بِجَمِيعِهِ؛ لِأَنَّهُ يَجْرِي مَجْرَى الكَفَّارَاتِ.

292. The prerequisites of *ṭawāf* are:

1. The intention.
2. To begin from the black stone.

- It is recommended to touch or kiss the stone.
- If one is unable to do that, one can raise their hand and make a gesture to it
- And say,

بِسْمِ اللهِ اللهُ أَكْبَرُ اللَّهُمَّ إِيْمَانًا بِكَ، وَتَصْدِيقًا بِكِتَابِكَ، ووَفَاءً بِعَهْدِكَ، واتِّبَاعًا لِسُنَّةِ نَبِيِّكَ مُحَمَّدٍ صَلَّى اللهُ عَلَيْهِ وَسَلَّمَ

Bismillāh, Allāhu Akbar, Allāhumma īmānan bika, wa taṣdīqan bi kitābik, wa wafāʾan biʿahdik, wat-tibāʿan li-sunnati nabiyyika Muḥammad.

3. The Kaʿbah should be to one's left.
4. One should complete seven circuits.
5. One has to be free from ritual and physical impurities.

293. To be in a state of purification for the other rites – other than *ṭawāf* - is recommended and not obligatory.

The Prophet ﷺ said, "The *ṭawāf* of the house is prayer (*ṣalāh*) except that Allāh سُبْحَانَهُ وَتَعَالَى has allowed one to speak during it."

٢٩٢. وَشُرُوطُ الطَّوَافِ مُطْلَقًا:

١. النِّيَّةُ

٢. وَالِابْتِدَاءُ بِهِ مِنْ الحَجَرِ

- وَيُسَنُّ أَنْ يَسْتَلِمَهُ وَيُقَبِّلَهُ،

- فَإِنْ لَمْ يَسْتَطِعْ أَشَارَ إِلَيْهِ،

- وَيَقُولُ عِنْدَ ذَلِكَ: بِسْمِ اللَّهِ اللَّهُ أَكْبَرُ، اللَّهُمَّ إِيمَانًا بِكَ، وَتَصْدِيقًا بِكِتَابِكَ، وَوَفَاءً بِعَهْدِكَ، وَاتِّبَاعًا لِسُنَّةِ نَبِيِّكَ مُحَمَّدٍ ﷺ

٣. وَأَنْ يَجْعَلَ البَيْتَ عَنْ يَسَارِهِ.

٤. وَيُكَمِّلَ الأَشْوَاطَ السَّبْعَةَ.

٥. وَأَنْ يَتَطَهَّرَ مِنْ الحَدَثِ وَالْخَبَثِ.

٢٩٣. وَالطِّهَارَةُ فِي سَائِرِ الأَنْسَاكِ -غَيْرَ الطَّوَافِ- سُنَّةٌ غَيْرُ وَاجِبَةٍ.

وَقَدْ وَرَدَ فِي الحَدِيثِ: «الطَّوَافُ بِالْبَيْتِ صَلَاةٌ، إِلَّا أَنَّ اللَّهَ أَبَاحَ فِيهِ الكَلَامَ.»

294. It is recommended to:

1. To do *iḍṭibāʿ* in the welcoming *ṭawāf*, which is to place the middle of the upper garment under the right armpit and the end of the garment on the left shoulder.
2. To lightly jog in the first three circuits during *ṭawāf*, and to walk the rest.

295. It is not recommended to run in the other types of *ṭawāf* or do *iḍṭibāʿ*.

296. The prerequisites for *saʿī* (running between *Ṣafā* & *Marwah*) are:

1. The intention.
2. To complete seven laps.
3. To start from *Ṣafā*.

297. One should remember Allāh ﷻ and call upon Him during *ṭawāf*, *saʿī* and the other rites due to the statement of the Prophet ﷺ, "Verily, the *ṭawāf* of the House, the *saʿī* between *Ṣafā* & *Marwah* and the throwing of stones at the *jimār* is for the establishment of the remembrance of Allāh ﷻ." (Aḥmad & Abū Dāwūd)

٢٩٤. وَسُنَّ

١. أن يَضْطَبِعَ فِي طَوَافِ الْقُدُومِ، بِأَنْ يَجْعَلَ وَسَطَ رِدَائِهِ تَحْتَ عَاتِقِهِ الأَيْمَنِ، وَطَرَفَهُ عَلَى عَاتِقِهِ الأَيْسَرِ،

٢. وَأَنْ يَرْمُلَ فِي الثَّلَاثَةِ الأَشْوَاطِ الأُوَلِ مِنْهُ، وَيَمْشِيَ فِي البَاقِي.

٢٩٥. وَكُلُّ طَوَافٍ سِوَى هَذَا لَا يُسَنُّ فِيهِ رمْلٌ وَلَا اِضْطِبَاعٌ.

٢٩٦. وَشُرُوطُ السَّعْيِ:

١. النِّيَّةُ،

٢. وَتَكْمِيلُ السَّبْعَةِ،

٣. وَالِابْتِدَاءُ مِنْ الصَّفَا.

٢٩٧. وَالْمَشْرُوعُ: أَنْ يُكْثِرَ الإِنْسَانُ فِي طَوَافِهِ وَسَعْيِهِ وَجَمِيعِ مَنَاسِكِهِ مِنْ ذِكْرِ اللَّهِ وَدُعَائِهِ؛ لِقَوْلِهِ ﷺ «إِنَّمَا جُعِلَ الطَّوَافُ بِالْبَيْتِ، وَبِالصَّفَا وَالمَرْوَةِ، وَرَمْيُ الجِمَارِ لِإِقَامَةِ ذِكْرِ اللَّهِ.»

298. Abū Hurayrah ؓ narrated that when Allāh ﷻ opened Makkah for the Prophet ﷺ:

He ﷺ stood amongst the people, praised and glorified Allāh ﷻ and said, "Verily Allāh ﷻ held back the elephant from Makkah and gave the domination of it to His Messenger and believers, and it (this territory) was not violable to anyone before me and it was made violable to me for an hour of a day, and it shall not be violable to anyone after me. So, neither molest the game, nor weed out thorns from it. And it is not lawful for anyone to pick up a thing dropped but one who makes public announcement of it. And if a relative of anyone is killed, he is entitled to opt for one of two things. Either he should be paid blood-money, or he can take life as (a just retribution). ʿAbbās ؓ said, "Allāh's Messenger, but what about *Idhkhir* (a kind of herbage), for we use it for our graves and for our houses? Whereupon Allāh's Messenger ﷺ said, "With the exception of *Idhkhir.*"" (Agreed upon).

299. The Prophet ﷺ said, "Mādīnah is sacred between *ʿAyr* until *Thawr.*" (Muslim)

300. The Prophet ﷺ said, "There are five creatures which are all evil, they are killed whether in the inviolable state or not: the crow, the kite, the scorpion, the mouse and the rabid dog." (Agreed upon)

٢٩٨. وعَنْ أَبِي هُرَيْرَةَ رَضِيَ اللهُ عَنْهُ قَالَ: «لَمَّا فَتَحَ اللَّهُ عَلَى رَسُولِهِ مَكَّةَ - قَامَ فِي النَّاسِ، فَحَمِدَ اللَّهَ، وَأَثْنَى عَلَيْهِ، ثُمَّ قَالَ: "إِنَّ اللَّهَ حَبَسَ عَنْ مَكَّةَ الفِيلَ، وَسَلَّطَ عَلَيْهَا رَسُولَهُ وَالْمُؤْمِنِينَ، وَإِنَّهَا لَمْ تَحِلَّ لِأَحَدٍ كَانَ قَبْلِي، وَإِنَّمَا أُحِلَّتْ لِي سَاعَةً مِنْ نَهَارٍ، وَإِنَّمَا لَنْ تَحِلَّ لِأَحَدٍ بَعْدِي: فَلَا يُنَفَّرُ صَيْدُهَا. وَلَا يُخْتَلَى شَوْكُهَا. وَلَا تَحِلُّ سَاقِطَتُهَا إِلَّا لِمُنْشِدٍ. وَمَنْ قُتِلَ لَهُ قَتِيلٌ فَهُوَ بِخَيْرِ النَّظَرَيْنِ. فَقَالَ العَبَّاسُ: إِلَّا الإِذْخِرَ يَا رَسُولَ اللَّهِ، فَإِنَّا نَجْعَلُهُ فِي قُبُورِنَا وَبُيُوتِنَا، فَقَالَ: إِلَّا الإِذْخِرَ.» مُتَّفَقٌ عَلَيْهِ.

٢٩٩. وَقَالَ صَلَّى اللهُ عَلَيْهِ وَسَلَّمَ: «المدِينَةُ حَرَمٌ مَا بَيْنَ عَيْرٍ إِلَى ثَوْرٍ.» رَوَاهُ مُسْلِمٌ

٣٠٠. وَقَالَ صَلَّى اللهُ عَلَيْهِ وَسَلَّمَ: «خَمْسٌ مِنْ الدَّوَابِ كُلُّهُنَّ فَاسِقٌ يُقْتَلْنَ فِي الحِلِّ والحَرَمِ: الغُرَابُ، والحَدَأَةُ، والعَقْرَبُ، والفَأْرَةُ، والكَلْبُ العَقُورُ.» مُتَّفَقٌ عَلَيْهِ

بَابُ الهَدْيِ والأُضْحِيَةِ والعَقِيقَة

Chapter: the *Hady*, *Uḍḥiyyah* & *ʿAqīqah*

301. It has already preceded what is obligatory for the *hady* (of *tamattuʿ* & *qirān*). Other than that, all other ritual sacrifices are recommended such as the *uḍḥiyyah* and *ʿaqīqah.*

302. It is not acceptable to give except:

1. A half-year-old lamb.
2. and *ath-thaniy* (which is):
- From camels, that which is five years old.
- From cows, that which is two years old.
- From goats, that which is one year old.

303. The Prophet ﷺ said, "Four (types of animals) are not acceptable for sacrifices:

1. A one-eyed animal which has clearly lost the sight of one eye,
2. A sick animal which is clearly sick,
3. A lame animal which clearly limps
4. And an animal with a broken leg with no marrow." (Reported by the five)

بَابُ الهَدْيِ وَالْأُضْحِيَّةِ وَالْعَقِيقَةِ

٣٠١. تَقَدَّمَ مَا يَجِبُ مِنَ الهَدْيِ، وَمَا سِوَاهُ سُنَّةٌ، وَكَذلِكَ الأُضْحِيَّةُ والعَقِيقَةُ.

٣٠٢. وَلَا يُجْزِئُ فِيهَا إِلَّا:

١. الجَذَعُ مِنَ الضَّأْنِ، وَهُوَ: مَا تَمَّ لَهُ نِصْفُ سَنَةٌ.

٢. وَالثَّنِيُّ.

- مِنْ الإِبِلِ: مَا لَهُ خَمْسُ سِنِينَ.
- وَمِنْ البَقَرِ: مَا لَهُ سَنَتَانِ.
- وَمِنْ المَعْزِ: مَا لَهُ سَنَةٌ.

٣٠٣. قَال ﷺ: «أَرْبَعٌ لَا تَجُوزُ فِي الأَضَاحِيّ:

١. العَوْرَاءُ البَيِّنُ عَوَرُهَا،

٢. وَالْمَرِيضَةُ البَيِّنُ مَرَضُهَا،

٣. وَالْعَرْجَاءُ البَيِّنُ ظَلْعُهَا،

٤. وَالْكَبِيرَة التِي لَا تُنْقِي.» صَحِيحٌ رَوَاهُ الخَمْسَةُ

304. The animal should be in a good state, free from defects. The more perfect the animal is, the more beloved it is to Allāh ﷻ and the more rewardable.

305. Jābir ؓ said, "We slaughtered with the Messenger of Allah ﷺ during the year of Al-Ḥudaibiyah: a camel for seven and a cow for seven." (Muslim)

306. It is recommended for the father to perform the *ʿaqīqah.*

307. Two sheep should be sacrificed if the newborn is a boy and one sheep if the new-born is a girl.

308. The Prophet ﷺ said, "The boy is mortgaged by his *ʿaqīqah*; slaughtering should be done for him on the seventh day, he should be given a name, and his head should be shaved." (Abū Dāwūd & Tirmidhi)

309. Some of the slaughtered meat should be eaten, some given away as a gift and some given away as charity.

310. The slaughterer should not be paid by giving him some of the meat; rather he should be given a gift or some charity.

End of volume one

٣٠٤. وَيَنْبَغِي أَنْ تَكُونَ كَرِيمَةً، كَامِلَةَ الصِّفَاتِ وَكُلَّمَا كَانَتْ أَكْمَلَ فَهِيَ أَحَبُّ إِلَى اللهِ، وَأَعْظَمُ لِأَجْرِ صَاحِبِهَا

٣٠٥. وَقَالَ جَابِرٌ: «نَحَرْنَا مَعَ النَّبِي صَلَّى اللهُ عَلَيْهِ وَسَلَّمَ عَامَ الْحُدَيْبِيَّةِ الْبُدْنَةَ عَنْ سَبْعَةٍ، وَالْبَقَرَةَ عَنْ سَبْعَةٍ.» رَوَاهُ مُسْلِمٌ.

٣٠٦. وَتُسَنُّ الْعَقِيقَةُ فِي حَقِّ الْأَبِ.

٣٠٧. عَنِ الْغُلَامِ شَاتَانِ، وَعَنِ الْجَارِيَةِ شَاةٌ.

٣٠٨. قَالَ ﷺ: «كُلُّ غُلَامٍ مُرْتَهَنٌ بِعَقِيقَتِهِ، تُذْبَحُ عِنْدَ يَوْمِ سَابِعِهِ، وَيُحْلَقُ وَيُسَمَّى.» صَحِيحٌ، رَوَاهُ الْخَمْسَةُ.

٣٠٩. وَيَأْكُلُ مِنَ الْمَذْكُورَاتِ، وَيُهْدِي، وَيَتَصَدَّقُ.

٣١٠. وَلَا يُعْطِي الْجَازِرَ أُجْرَتَهُ مِنْهَا بَلْ يُعْطِيهِ هَدِيَّةً أَوْ صَدَقَةً.

Bibliography

قائمة المراجع

Al Saᶜdi, ᶜAbd al Raḥmān bin Nāṣir. *Manhaj al Sālikīn*. Riyāḍ: Dār ibn al Jawzi, 2003.

Al Jibrīn, ᶜAbd Allāh bin ᶜAbd al Raḥmān. *Ibhāj al Muʾminīn bi-Sharḥ Manhaj al Sālikīn*. Riyāḍ: Madār al Waṭan, 2001.

Qalᶜaji, Muḥammad Rawwās. *Muᶜjam Lughah al Fuqahāʾ*. Beirut: Dār al Nafāʾis, 1996.

Printed in Great Britain
by Amazon

34060098R00138